SOHO THEATRE IN A CO-PRODUCTION
WITH THE BELGRADE THEATRE COVENTRY PRESENT

BEHUD

(Beyond Belief)

Written by **Gurpreet Kaur Bhatti**
Directed by **Lisa Goldman**

Behud is presented as the David Aukin Commission in recognition
of his continuing contribution to the Company in the 10th anniversary
of Soho Theatre's Dean Street home.

First performed at The Belgrade Theatre Coventry on 27 March 2010

Soho Theatre is supported by ACE, Bloomberg, John Ellerman Foundation,
TEQUILA\London, Westminster City Council, The City Bridge Trust

Performances in the Lorenz Auditorium

Registered Charity No: 267234

Soho Theatre in a co-production
with The Belgrade Theatre Coventry present

BEHUD

(Beyond Belief)

by Gurpreet Kaur Bhatti

Cast

Tarlochan Kaur Grewal	**Chetna Pandya**
DCI Vincent Harris/Andrew Fleming	**John Hodgkinson**
DI Gurpal (Gary) Singh Mangat/Khushwant Singh Bains	**Avin Shah**
Satinder Shergill/Girl (Baby)	**Priyanga Burford**
Mr Sidhu	**Ravin J Ganatra**
Amrik/Man	**Shiv Grewal**
Joanne Stevenson	**Lucy Briers**

Writer	**Gurpreet Kaur Bhatti**
Director	**Lisa Goldman**
Designer	**Hannah Clark**
Lighting Designer	**Richard G Jones**
Sound Designer	**Matt McKenzie**
Movement Director	**Ann Yee**
Projection Design	**Douglas O'Connell**

Production Manager	**Matt Noddings**
Stage Manager	**Emma McKie**
Deputy Stage Manager	**Sarah Caselton-Smith**
Assistant Stage Manager	**Kathryn Linnell**
Wardrobe Supervisor	**Liz Evans**
Fight Director	**Bret Yount**
Dialect Coach	**Jan Haydn Rowles**
Casting Director	**Nadine Rennie** cᴅɢ

Lisa Goldman and Gurpreet Kaur Bhatti would like to give a very special thanks to Nick Hytner and all at the National Theatre Studio and to Kerry Michael and all at Theatre Royal Stratford East for their generous support of **Behud** during 2009, for enabling us to develop the play further through rehearsed readings, and for their brilliant feedback.

Cast and Creative Biographies

LUCY BRIERS JOANNE STEVENSON

Lucy trained at Bristol Old Vic Theatre School.

Theatre includes: *Bedroom Farce* and *Miss Julie* (Rose Theatre, Kingston); *Private Fears In Public Places* and *Just Between Ourselves* (Theatre Royal, Northampton); *Ivanov* (Donmar Warehouse, London); *Sexual Perversity In Chicago* (Norwich Playhouse); *Some Kind Of Bliss* (Trafalgar Studios / Brits off Broadway – What's On Stage Best Solo Performer Nominee 2008); *The Voysey Inheritance* (National Theatre, London); *Musik* (The Arcola, London); *Cloud Nine* and *Teeth 'N' Smiles* (Crucible Theatre, Sheffield); *Electra* (Gate Theatre, London); *As You Like It* (Crucible Theatre, Sheffield and Lyric Theatre, Hammersmith); *The Winter's Tale* (Southwark Playhouse); *Henry IV Parts I And II* (National Tour and Old Vic) and *The Entertainer* (Birmingham Rep).

Television includes: *Ashes to Ashes*; *Einstein and Eddington*; *Rough Crossings*; *Doctors*; *Silent Witness*; *Broken News*; *Bodies*; *Wives and Daughters*; *Game On*; *Pride and Prejudice*; *Red Dwarf* (BBC); *Bonkers* (ITV); *Poirot* (Granada) and *Genie in the House* (Nickelodeon).

Film includes: *The Children of Men*.
Radio includes: *With Great Pleasure*; *The Making of a Marchioness*; *Zazie Dans Le Metro*; *The Recruiting Officer*; *Henry IV Parts I and II* and *Last of the Barsetshire Chronicles* (BBC).

PRIYANGA BURFORD SATINDER SHERGILL / GIRL (BABY)

Theatre includes: *On Religion* (Soho Theatre); *The White Devil* (InService Productions, Brighton); *A Passage To India* (Shared Experience); *A Midsummer Night's Dream* (RSC); *Twelfth Night* (Liverpool Playhouse); *Arabian Nights* (International Tour); *The Ballad of Yachiyo* (Gate Theatre) and *The John Wayne Principle* (Nuffield Theatre, Southampton).

Film credits includes: *The Other Man* (Rainmark Films) and *Magicians* (Objective Productions).

Television includes: *Married Single Other* (Left Bank Pictures); *The Commander: The Fraudster* (La Plante Productions); *Dalziel & Pascoe, Extras and Casualty* (BBC); *Murphy's Law* (Tiger Aspect); *Heartless* (Ecosse); *Holby City* (BBC); *Trial By Fire* (ITV); *A Rather English Marriage* (Winner of BAFTA award for Best Single Drama, BBC / Wall To Wall) and *The Vice* (ITV).

Priyanga has also recorded numerous radio plays and was the Winner of the 1998 Carlton Hobbs BBC Radio Competition.

RAVIN J GANATRA MR SIDHU

Ravin trained at The Manchester School of Theatre at Manchester Metropolitan University.

Theatre includes: *Zameen* (Kali Theatre, London); *Bombay Dreams* (Really Useful Group, London and West End); *Passage to India* (Shared Experience); *Hamlet* and *The Winter's Tale* (Library Theatre, Manchester); The Shakespeare Globe Fellowship 2002; *Journey to the West Trilogy* (Tara Arts) and *The Mahabharata Trilogy* (YOMT).

Film and TV includes: *The Infidel* (Revolver Entertainment); *Dappers* and *Handle With Prayer* (BBC); *Britz* (Mentorn TV); *Torchwood (BBC)* and *The Bill* (ITV); *Coronation Street* (Granada); *Holby City, Eastenders, Waterloo Road* and *Doctors* (BBC); *Prime Suspect 5* (Granada); *Nighty Night* (BBC); *Entrapment* (20th Century Fox) and *Tom and Thomas* (Universal).

Radio credits include: Playing the recurring character, Uncle Jai on BBC Asian Network *Silver Street* and numerous characters for BBC Radio 4 Drama.

SHIV GREWAL AMRIK/MAN

Theatre includes: *A British Subject* (59E59 Theatre, New York and Edinburgh); *The Good Soul of Szechuan* (Young Vic, London); *Rafta Rafta* and *Tiger at the Gate* (National Theatre, London); *Too Close to Home* (Manchester Library Theatre and Lyric Theatre Hammersmith); *Gladiator Games* (Crucible Theatre, Sheffield and Theatre Royal Stratford East); *A Fine Balance* (Hampstead Theatre); *Twelfth Night* (Albery Theatre, London); *Strictly Dandia* (Edinburgh International Festival); *Balti Kings* (West Yorkshire Playhouse); *Café Vesuvio* (Manchester Royal Exchange); *A Midsummer Night's Dream* (Tara Arts and London Bubble Theatre); *Othello* (Wales Actors' Company) and *A Streetcar Named Desire* (Sherman Theatre, Cardiff).

Film and television includes: *Brothers in Trouble; My Son the Fanatic; The James Gang; Felicia's Journey; A Quiet Desperation; The Vanguard; Messiah 3* (BBC); *Second Generation* (Channel 4); *When You Are Ready Mr McGill* (ITV); *In a Land Of Plenty, Doctors,*

Holby City, EastEnders and Slings and Arrows (BBC) and *The Bill* and *Trial Of Gemma Lang* (ITV).

Radio includes: *The Archers; Westway; Silver Street; Book at Bed Time* and *Book of the Week*. He has also been a member of the BBC Radio Drama Company.

JOHN HODGKINSON DCI VINCENT HARRIS/ANDREW FLEMING

Theatre includes: *The Winter's Tale* (Headlong Tour); *His Dark Materials* (Birmingham Rep); *Aristo* (Chichester); *Hapgood* (Birmingham Rep and West Yorkshire Playhouse); *Absurdia* (Donmar Warehouse); *Uncle Vanya* (Birmingham Rep); *The Eleventh Capital* (The Royal Court); *The Taming of the Shrew* and *A Midsummer Night's Dream* (Regent's Park Open Air); *A Journey to London* (Orange Tree Theatre); *Neville's Island* (Birmingham Rep); *I Have Been Here Before* (Watford Palace); *Arcadia* (Bristol Old Vic); *The Two Gentlemen of Verona* (Regent's Park Open Air); *The Hare Trilogy* (Birmingham Rep); *Romeo and Juliet, As You Like It* and *Oh What A Lovely War* (Regent's Park Open Air); *Alice in Wonderland* and *Alice Through the Looking Glass* (RSC); *The Front Page* (The Donmar Warehouse); *Le Bourgeois Gentilhomme* (Edinburgh Festival); *Good Morning Bill* (Scala Stockholm); *The Visit* (Chichester); *The Seagull* (Royal National Theatre); *London Assurance* (Chichester / West End); *Love's Labour's Lost* (Chichester); *Cardboard City* (Soho Poly and Tour); *Love's Labour's Lost, A Jovial Crew, The Beggar's Opera, The Winter's Tale, Dr Jekyll and Mr Hyde, The Pretenders, Richard II, Edward II* and *Comedy of Errors* (RSC) and *Events*

Whilst Guarding Bofors Gun and Leocadia (RSC Festival).
Film and television includes: Thunderpants (Dragon Pictures); Firelight (Carnival Films); Whatever Happened to Harold Smith? (West Eleven Films); Criminal Justice (BBC); Heartbeat (ITV); Broken News, Doctors and Brief Encounters (BBC); Peep Show (Series 1 and 2 – Channel 4); EastEnders and My Family (BBC); The Lee Evans Show, Holby City and Chambers (BBC); The Bill (Pearson); The Estate Agents (Angel Eye / Channel 4); People Like Us (BBC); Kiss Me Kate (Carlton); The Peter Principle (Hat Trick); Pure Wickedness (BBC); Boyz Unlimited (Hat Trick); Then (Junction 5 / Channel 4); Keeping Mum (BBC); Duck Patrol (LWT); Dad (BBC); Sometime Never (Select TV) and Inside Victor Lewis Smith (BBC).

CHETNA PANDYA TARLOCHAN KAUR GREWAL

Chetna recently appeared in Shades at the Royal Court, which was the recipient of a Critic's Circle Award. She also took part in the international tour of A Disappearing Number with Simon McBurney's Theatre Complicite. That play was the recipient of The Evening Standard Theatre Award, Critics' Circle Award and the Olivier Award for Best Play. In 2009 Chetna co-founded Outspoken Arts, a partnership that offers bespoke creative workshops for mainstream and marginalized youth and community groups.
Theatre includes: Arabian Nights (RSC); Behud (Rehearsed reading – Central Lines, Theatre Royal Stratford East); The Spiral and Shades (Royal Court Theatre, London); A Disappearing Number (Complicite /

Barbican Theatre); Unheard Voices (Royal Court Theatre, London); Future Perfect (Shakespeare's Globe); Deadeye (Kali Theatre Company/ Birmingham Rep and onto Soho Theatre); The Coram Boy (Royal National Theatre Olivier); Lucky Stiff (Lucky Stuff Productions); Romeo and Juliet (Changeling Theatre Company/ tour) and Kali Futures (Kali Theatre Company).
Film and television includes: Identity (ITV); Holby Blue, Broken News and The Worst Week of My Life (BBC); Green Wing (Channel Four) and The Message, New Tricks and Doctors (BBC).
Radio includes: A Disappearing Number and Bora Bistrah (BBC Radio Three) and Bitter Fruits of Palestine.

AVIN SHAH DI GURPAL (GARY) SINGH MANGAT/ KHUSHWANT SINGH BAINS

Theatre includes: The Island Princess, Edward III, Eastward Ho!, and The Malcontent (RSC); Bollywood Jane (West Yorkshire Playhouse); Touched (Edinburgh Fringe); Romeo & Juliet (Royal Exchange, Manchester); Office (Edinburgh Lyceum & Soho Theatre); East is East (New Vic, Stoke) and The Crutch (Royal Court).
Television include: Eastenders, Karim's Story, The Bill, Jane Hall's Big Bad Bus Ride, Doctors, Casualty, Life As We Know It, Hope & Glory and Hetty Wainthrop Investigates.
Film includes: The Land of the Blind, Dead Meat, Brothers in Trouble, The Apology, Crossing Bridges, Thicker than Water and Contagious.

GURPREET KAUR BHATTI
WRITER
Gurpreet Kaur Bhatti's first play

Behsharam (Shameless) broke box office records when it played at Soho Theatre and the Birmingham Rep in 2001. Her play Behzti (Dishonour) was sensationally closed in December 2004, after playing to packed houses at the Birmingham Rep. In 2005 Behzti won the prestigious Susan Smith Blackburn Prize for the best English language play written by a woman. In 2006 the play was translated into French and did sell-out tours in France and Belgium. She is now writing a feature film for Stealth Films, an adaptation of An Enemy of the People for the BBC World Service, working on stage commissions for Kali Theatre, Tara Arts and Birmingham Rep, as well as developing a television series for the BBC and a play for the National Theatre Studio.

Other credits include the half hour film Dead Meat, produced by Channel 4 as part of the Dogma TV season; Stitched Up (commissioned series for BBC1); Honour (single film for BBC2); The Cleaner, an hour-long film for BBC1; Pound Shop Boys (originally commissioned by October Films/Film Council/Scottish Screen and developed through PAL); Lipstick And Nails (police drama for Great Meadow Productions); Pile Up and The Bride (both commissioned serials for Carlton Television); Two Old Ladies (Leicester Haymarket); Airport 2000 (Leicester Haymarket/Riverside Studios); Londonee (Theatre Royal Stratford East – rehearsed reading); Mera Des (My Country), a fifty minute play for Radio 3; My Lithuanian Lady (BBC World Service); over thirty episodes of the BBC World Service Drama Serial – Westway (1999-2001); and nine episodes of Eastenders (2001-2005).

LISA GOLDMAN DIRECTOR

Behud will be Lisa's final play as Artistic Director of Soho Theatre. Previous new plays developed and directed for Soho Theatre include Natasha Langridge's Shraddha; a first theatrical response to the economic crisis called Everything Must Go by writers including Bola Agbaje, Paula Stanic, Megan Barker, Oladipo Agboluaje, Will Eno; Maxwell Golden, Marisa Carnesky and Steve Thompson; This Isn't Romance by In-Sook Chappell (winner of Verity Bargate Award) and Piranha Heights by Philip Ridley. Other directing credits include Baghdad Wedding by Hassan Abdulrazzak (which Lisa also directed as a Radio 3 Sunday play and won the 2008 George Devine and Meyer Whitworth Awards for Best New Play) and A Couple of Poor, Polish-Speaking Romanians by Dorota Maslowska, which Lisa also co-translated with Paul Sirett. Her first play for the company was Leaves of Glass, also by Philip Ridley.

Lisa was previously founding Artistic Director of The Red Room, for whom new writing credits include writing and directing the site-specific walkabout, Hoxton Story; The Bogus Woman (Fringe First and Manchester Evening News Award – Bush Theatre, / Traverse Theatre / tour / Radio 3 Sunday play); Bites (Bush Theatre), Animal (Soho Theatre) and Hanging (CBL Radio 4 Friday play) all by Kay Adshead; Sunspots, The Shorewatchers' House, Know Your Rights and People on the River all by Judy Upton; Ex, Obsession and Surfing (Critics' Choice seasons at BAC) and the 35mm short film My Sky is Big (NFT1 and festivals) all by Rob Young; Seeing Red, a two month festival of dissent by 16 writers (BAC);

Made in England by Parv Bancil (BAC) and *Playing Fields* by Neela Dolezalova (Soho Theatre). Lisa's producing collaboration with Anthony Neilson enabled the creation of *The Censor* and *Stitching* (Time Out Live Awards 1997 and 2003) and *The Night Before Christmas*.

HANNAH CLARK DESIGNER

Hannah trained in theatre design at Nottingham Trent University and Central School of Speech and Drama. She was a winner of the 2005 Linbury Biennial Prize for stage design. Designs include: *Gambling* (Soho Theatre); *Eigengrau* and *2nd MAY 1997* (The Bush); *A Midsummer Night's Dream* (The Globe); *Knives In Hens*, *Thyestes* and *Torn* (Arcola); *Under Milk Wood* (Northampton Theatre Royal); *Nocturnal* and *Big Love* (The Gate); *Billy Wonderful* (Liverpool Everyman); *Company* and *Hortensia and the Museum of Dreams* (RADA); *The Snow Queen* (West Yorkshire Playhouse); *Proper Clever* (Liverpool Playhouse); *Pequenas Delicias* and *Roadkill Cafe* (Requardt & Company, Centro Coreográfico de Montemor-o-Novo, Portugal / Teatro Fondamenta Nuove, Venice / The Place); *House of Agnes* (Paines Plough); *Breakfast With Mugabe* (Theatre Royal Bath); *The Cracks In My Skin* and *Who's Afraid of Virginia Woolf?* (Manchester Royal Exchange); *Othello* (Salisbury Playhouse); *As You Like It* and *We That Are Left* (Watford Palace Theatre); *Terre Haute* (Assembly Rooms, Edinburgh / Trafalgar Studios / UK Tour / 59E59, New York); *The Taming of the Shrew* (Bristol Old Vic) and *Jammy Dodgers* (Requardt & Company, The Place / Royal Opera House 2 / INT Tour).

RICHARD G JONES LIGHTING DESIGNER

Richard is currently working on *The Railway Children* (to take place in the old Eurostar terminal at Waterloo station over the summer); *City Of Angels* (for The Bridewell Theatre) and *Copacabana* (for the Watermill Theatre in Newbury).
Theatre includes: Richard designed the lighting for *Sweeney Todd* at the Eugene O'Neill Theatre in New York, for which he won The Drama Desk Award for Outstanding Lighting and was nominated for an Outer Circle Critics award. Richard was also nominated for a Theatrical Management Association award for Best Lighting Design for *The Railway Children* for York Theatre Royal at the National Railway Museum. Other recent lighting designs include: *Canterbury Tales* (Northern Broadsides); *The Dumb Waiter* and *A Kind of Alaska* (Derby LIVE); *Twelfth Night*, *The Homecoming* and *Up The Duff* (York Theatre Royal); *Sunset Boulevard* and *The Hot Mikado* (Watermill Theatre, on tour and in the West End); *Spongebob Squarepants: The Sponge That Could Fly!* (UK and South African 2009 tour); *Horrid Henry Live* and *Horrid* (West End and UK 2009 tour) and *Ich war noch niemals in New York* (Operettanhaus in Hamburg, Germany).

MATT MCKENZIE SOUND DESIGNER

Matt McKenzie came to the UK from New Zealand in 1978. He toured with *Paines Plough* before joining the staff at the Lyric Theatre, Hammersmith in 1979. He designed the sound for several of their productions including *Favourite Nights, Rents, Brittanicus,*

Noises Off, The White Glove, The Provoked Wife, Private Dick, Miss Julie, Hobson's Choice, Mass Appeal, Crime and Punishment, Lent and The Man Who Fell in Love with His Wife. Since joining Autograph in 1984, Matt has been responsible for the sound design for Macbeth (Nuffield Theatre, Southampton); Una Pooka (The Tricyle, London); Angry Housewives, The Hypochondriac, Faith Hope and Charity, Sailor Beware, Loot, Lady Audley's Secret, Madras House, The Way of the World, Ghost Train, Greasepaint, In the Summer House and Exact Change (Lyric Theatre, Hammersmith); Vertigo, That Good Night and The Hinge of the World (Yvonne Arnaud Theatre, Guildford); Saturday Sunday Monday, Easy Virtue, The Seagull, A Midsummer Night's Dream, Master and Margarita, 5/11 and Nicholas Nickleby (Chichester Festival Theatre); The Giant (Hampstead Theatre, London); Three Sisters on Hope Street (Liverpool Everyman); Dracula, Frankenstein, A Midsummer Night's Dream and Macbeth (Derby Playhouse); Flamingos, Damages, After The End and tHedYsFUnCKshOnalZ (Bush Theatre, London); Wuthering Heights (Birmingham Rep).

Matt's work in the West End includes Made in Bangkok, The House of Bernarda Alba, A Piece of My Mind, Journey's End, A Madhouse in Goa, Barnaby and the Old Boys, Irma Vep, Gasping, Map of the Heart, Tango Argentino, When She Danced, Misery, Murder Is Easy, The Odd Couple, Pygmalion, Things We Do For Love, Long Day's Journey Into Night, Macbeth, Sexual Perversity in Chicago, Calico, A Life in the Theatre,

Swimming With Sharks, Nicholas Nickleby, Deep Blue Sea, Female of the Species, Girl With A Pearl Earring. Matt's work for Sir Peter Hall includes Lysistrata, The Master Builder, School for Wives, Mind Millie for Me, A Streetcar Named Desire, Three of a Kind, Amadeus (West End and Broadway); the opening season at Soho Theatre and several subsequent productions including Leaves of Glass and Baghdad Wedding; Frame312, After Miss Julie and Days of Wine and Roses (Donmar Warehouse, London); The Giant and 3 Sisters on Hope Street (Hampstead) and Iron, The People Next Door and Orphans (Traverse Theatre, Edinburgh).

He was Sound Supervisor for the Peter Hall Seasons at The Old Vic and The Piccadilly and designed the sound for Waste, Cloud 9, The Seagull, The Provok'd Wife, King Lear, The Misanthrope, Major Barbara, Filumena and Kafka's Dick. Work for the RSC includes Family Reunion, Henry V, The Duchess of Mafli, Hamlet, The Lieutenant of Inishmore, Julius Caesar and A Midsummer Night's Dream. Matt's musical work includes Love off the Shelf (Nuffield Theatre, Southampton); The Bells are Ringing and Talk of the Steamie (Greenwich Theatre, London); Forbidden Broadway and Blues in the Night (West End); Matthew Bourne's Car Man (West End and International Tour); Putting It Together, The Gondoliers, How to Succeed in Business Without Really Trying, Carousel, Babes In Arms, Funny Girl, Music Man and Oklahoma (Chichester Festival Theatre); Oh What A Lovely War, A Christmas Carol, Sweeney Todd, Company, Into The Woods, Merrily We Roll Along and Moon Landing for Derby Playhouse;

Annie Get Your Gun (Young Vic, London); Mark Ravenhill's *Dick Whittington* for the Barbican and the co-sound design of *Tess of the D'Urbervilles* at the Savoy and *Alice in Wonderland* for the RSC.

ANN YEE MOVEMENT DIRECTOR

Theatre credits as movement director include: *King Lear* (RSC); *The Secret Garden* (West Yorkshire Playhouse); *Dance Radio* (Roundhouse); *Shraddha* (Soho Theatre, London); *Mates* (part of the new writing collective, DryWrite at Latitude Festival); *Much Ado About Nothing* (Regent's Park Open Air Theatre); *This Isn't Romance* (Soho Theatre, London); *Eric's* (Liverpool Everyman); *Romeo and Juliet* (Middle Temple Hall, London); *Oxford Street* (Royal Court Theatre, London); *Hamlet* (Theater Rozmaitosci, Warsaw); *The Lion, The Witch and The Wardrobe* (West Yorkshire Playhouse and Birmingham Rep); *Bad Girls The Musical* (Garrick Theatre, London); *Angels in America* (Lyric Theatre, Hammersmith and UK tour); *Bent* (Trafalgar Studios, London); *Hair* (Gate Theatre, London); *Woyzeck* (St. Ann's Warehouse, New York and Gate Theatre, London); *The Odyssey* (Lyric Theatre, Hammersmith and Bristol Old Vic); *The Magic Carpet* (Lyric Theatre, Hammersmith); *Big Love* (Gate Theatre, London); *Food* (Traverse Theatre, Edinburgh and UK tour) and *Sex, Chips and Rock and Roll* (Royal Exchange Theatre, Manchester).

DOUGLAS O'CONNELL
PROJECTION DESIGN

Douglas is a Post Graduate Senior Lecturer in The Visual Language of Performance at Wimbledon College of Art in London, where he was awarded a fellowship for Promising New Research. In addition he is a Visiting Lecturer and Strand tutor at the Central School of Speech and Drama. Douglas began his career working in Off Broadway and regional theatre throughout New York. As a member of Redmoon Theatre in Chicago, he received awards in design for his work at the renowned Steppenwolf Studio Theater.

Now based in the UK, he has been lead artist on numerous site specific projects that have included work with the Birmingham Royal Ballet, Collective Art Noise, Emergency Exit Arts and the Greenwich/Dockland Festival. Recently Douglas was commissioned to design a video birthday card to commemorate the 50th Anniversary of Harold Pinter's *The Birthday Party*, which was featured at the 50th Anniversary Gala and now resides as part of the Pinter collection at the British Library.

Recent projection and video credits include:

Here's What I Did With My Body Did One Day (National Tour); *Back At You* (Lightwork/Battersea Arts Centre); *Sarajevo Story* (Lyric Theatre, Hammersmith Studio); *Saturday Night Sunday Morning* (Harrogate Theatre, London); *Fight Face* by Sophie Wooley (Lyric Theatre, Hammersmith Studio); *This Isn't Romance* (Soho Theatre, London); *Monsters* (Arcola); *Dance Marathon* (Vancouver Winter Olympics) and *Ballet Shoes* (Peacock Theatre, London).

PERFORMANCE PROVOCATIVE AND COMPELLING THEATRE, COMEDY AND CABARET
SOHO CONNECT A THRIVING EDUCATION, COMMUNITY AND OUTREACH PROGRAMME
WRITERS' CENTRE DISCOVERING AND NURTURING NEW WRITERS AND ARTISTS
SOHO THEATRE BAR OPEN UNTIL LATE. TICKETHOLDERS GET 10% OFF SELECTED FOOD AND DRINK

'The invaluable Soho Theatre'
MICHAEL BILLINGTON, THE GUARDIAN

'The capital's centre for daring international drama.'
EVENING STANDARD

'A jewel in the West End'
BBC LONDON

THE TERRACE BAR
Drinks can be taken into the auditorium and are available from the Terrace Bar on the second floor.

SOHO THEATRE ONLINE
Giving you the latest information and previews of upcoming shows, Soho Theatre can be found on facebook, twitter and youtube as well as at sohotheatre.com

EMAIL INFORMATION LIST
For regular programme updates and offers visit sohotheatre.com/mailing

HIRING THE THEATRE
Soho Theatre has a range of rooms and spaces for hire. Please contact the theatre on 020 7287 5060 or go to sohotheatre.com/hires for further details.

Soho Theatre is supported by:

ACE, Bloomberg, John Ellerman Foundation, TEQUILA\London, Westminster City Council, The City Bridge Trust

Performances in the Lorenz Auditorium / Registered Charity No: 267234

$OHO STAFF

Artistic Director: Lisa Goldman
Executive Director: Mark Godfrey

BOARD OF DIRECTORS

Nicholas Allott (chair)
Sue Robertson (vice chair)
David Aukin
Oladipo Agboluaje
Norma Heyman
Shappi Khorsandi
Jeremy King
Lynne Kirwin
Neil Mendoza
David Pelham
Carolyn Ward
Roger Wingate

HONORARY PATRONS

Bob Hoskins - President
Peter Brook CBE
Simon Callow
Gurinder Chadha
Sir Richard Eyre CBE

ARTISTIC TEAM

Writers' Centre Director   Nina Steiger
Soho Connect Director   Suzanne Gorman
Casting Director   Nadine Rennie
Producer – Late Night Programme   Steve Lock
Writers' Centre Assistant   Alix Thorpe
International Associate   Paul Sirett

ADMINISTRATION

General Manager   Erin Gavaghan
PA to Directors   Amanda Joy
Financial Controller   Kevin Dunn
Finance Officer   Kate Wickens

MARKETING, DEVELOPMENT AND PRESS

Communications Director	Jacqui Gellman
Development Director	Jo Cottrell
Development Consultant	Elizabeth Duducu
Marketing Manager	Nicki Marsh
Press and Public Relations	Fiona McCurdy
(020 7478 0142)	
Marketing & Digital Officer	Alexander Fleming
Development Assistant	Tristan Bernays
Access Officer	Charlie Swinbourne
Marketing Intern	Vikki Mizon

BOX OFFICE AND FRONT OF HOUSE

Front of House and Events Manager Jennifer Dromey
Box Office Supervisor Natalie Worrall

Box Office Assistants Danielle Baker, Lou Beere,
Amanda Collins, Philip Elvy,
Tamsin Flessey, Lynne Forbes,
Louise Green, Eniola Jaiyeoba,
Helen Matthews, Leah Read, Becca Savory,
Will Sherriff-Hammond, Dominique Trotter
and Tom Webb.

Duty Managers Julia Haworth, Tara Kane
and Martin Murphy.

Front of House staff Emma Akwafo, Celyn Ebenezer,
Stephen Hoo, Ian Irvine, Kyle Jenkins,
Bea Kempton, James Mann,
Mark McManus, Marta Moroni
and James Munroe.

PRODUCTION

Production Manager	Matt Noddings
Technical Manager	Nick Blount
Head of Lighting	Christoph Wagner
Technician	Natalie Smith

21 Dean Street,
London W1D 3NE
sohotheatre.com
Admin 020 7287 5060
Box Office 020 7478 0100

The Soho Theatre Development Campaign

The Soho Theatre Development Campaign

Soho Theatre receives core funding from Arts Council England, London. In order to provide as diverse a programme as possible and expand our audience development and outreach work, we rely upon additional support from trusts, foundations, individuals and businesses.

All of our major sponsors share a common commitment to developing new areas of activity and encouraging creative partnerships between business and the arts. We are immensely grateful for the invaluable support from our sponsors and donors and wish to thank them for their continued commitment.

Soho Theatre has a Friends Scheme in support of its education programme and work developing new writers and reaching new audiences.

To find out how to become a Friend of Soho Theatre, contact the development department on 020 7478 0111, or visit sohotheatre.com.

Principal Sponsors and Education Patrons:

Anonymous
BBC Children in Need
Bloomberg
Capita
The City Bridge Trust
John Ellerman Foundation
Esmée Fairbairn Foundation
Financial Express
St. Giles-in-the-Fields Parochial Charities
The Groucho Club
Smee Family Interests
TEQUILA\London
The Rose Foundation
Carolyn Ward
The Harold Hyam Wingate Foundation

In-Kind Sponsors:

Latham & Watkins
Roscolab Ltd

Belgrade Theatre Coventry

The Belgrade Theatre was built in 1958 as part of the reconstruction of Coventry after World War II. Holding 858 in its two-tier main auditorium, it remains one of the largest regional producing theatres in Britain.

The Theatre soon became renowned for its programme of exciting new drama and early Company members at the Belgrade included Trevor Nunn, Ian McKellen, Joan Plowright and Leonard Rossiter, with Arnold Wesker and David Turner among the new dramatists.

The Theatre remains the major arts and cultural facility in Coventry and the only building-based professional producing theatre company in the city.

Having started the Theatre-in-Education (TIE) movement in the 1960s the Belgrade also continues to pioneer new initiatives in this field as well as other community and outreach programmes.

The current Artistic Director and Chief Executive, Hamish Glen, was appointed to the theatre in March 2003, bringing with him a new commitment to restore the Belgrade Theatre's reputation as a high quality producing house.

Autumn 2007 saw the re-opening of the Belgrade after completion of its major capital project, including the creation of a new, flexible 250 seat second space, B2, and refurbishment of the existing listed building.

Since re-opening, the reinvigorated Belgrade has produced numerous successful productions including Joanna Murray-Smith's adaptation of Ingmar Bergman's *Scenes from a Marriage*, directed by Trevor Nunn, and Alan Pollock's play about the Coventry Blitz, *One Night in November*, directed by Hamish Glen.

For further information please visit www.belgrade.co.uk

Belgrade Management Team

Artistic Director	**Hamish Glen**
Executive Director	**Joanna Reid**
Chairman of the Board of Directors	**David Shortland**
Director of Production	**John Miller**
Technical Director	**Mark Davies**
Director of Communications	**Nicola Young**
Communications Manager	**Ray Clenshaw**
Associate Director, Community and Education	**Justine Theman**
General Manager, Community and Education	**Janthi Mills**
Head of Development	**David Jane**
Financial Controller	**Nigel Vasey**

BEHUD (BEYOND BELIEF)

Gurpreet Kaur Bhatti

BEHUD (BEYOND BELIEF)

OBERON BOOKS
LONDON

First published in 2010 by Oberon Books Ltd
521 Caledonian Road, London N7 9RH

A catalogue record for this book is available from the British Library.

ISBN: 978-1-84943-096-8

Cover design by Hugo Glendinning

This one's for Michael

Huge thanks to the many people who have offered
support and encouragement during the last five years.
To my family and friends whose enduring love and
faith have sustained me through both the dark and the
light. To the amazing Cathy King for her dedication
and ferocity; and Robert and Mady for their hard work.
To everyone at Soho Theatre, especially Nina Steiger
for her clever eye. To Hamish Glen and all at Coventry
Belgrade for believing in the piece and finally to the
very special Lisa Goldman whose passion and integrity
have brought about this production.

'Art is the lie that reveals the truth'
Pablo Picasso

Characters

TARLOCHAN KAUR GREWAL
Playwright

DCI VINCENT HARRIS
A man unhinged

DI GURPAL (GARY) SINGH MANGAT
An all too decent individual

SATINDER (SAT) SHERGILL
A ravenous reporter

MR SIDHU
An overly successful businessman

AMRIK
A man to whom life has not been kind

KHUSHWANT SINGH BAINS
An energised adolescent
(Performed by actor playing GARY)

ANDREW FLEMING
Artistic Director of the Writers' Theatre
(Performed by actor playing VINCE)

JOANNE STEVENSON
Deputy Leader of the local Council

GIRL (BABY)
A cheeky slip of a thing, aged 10
(Performed by actor playing SAT)

MAN
Just over from the Punjab, aged 23
(Performed by actor playing AMRIK)

Prologue

Dawn. The stage is black. The lights go up slowly to reveal an Asian woman, TARLOCHAN, lying on the floor in front of a plain desk and chair in a huge stark white space. There is a red notebook and a filthy old bargain bucket of KFC by her side. At first sight she could be dead but she starts to move and eventually gets up, picks up the notebook and sits at the desk. She's a frumpy, dumpy specimen wearing an oversized hoodie and baggy tracksuit bottoms. TARLOCHAN produces a pen and starts to write in the red notebook. Moments pass. She stops writing and looks towards stage right. DI GURPAL (GARY) SINGH MANGAT, a broad, handsome sixfooter with impressionable eyes and a too-open face enters from stage right, he is carrying a fat script. It is as though he hasn't seen TARL, like she doesn't exist. GARY sits down at the desk and starts to read the script he is carrying. While he studies it he scribbles on a pad. TARL gets up and watches him.

GARY: Ugh.

DCI VINCENT (VINCE) HARRIS enters carrying a briefcase and a flipchart. VINCE is the Head of the Community Safety Unit and is a wiry, college-educated copper. He sets up the flipchart. Again the characters do not notice/acknowledge TARL. GARY'S face becomes further gnarled with distaste.

GARY: It's making me feel sick.

VINCE: Pull yourself together you skinny homosexual.

TARL: Language!

VINCE: Pull yourself together you bloody blouse.

Smartly dressed in a sharp suit, VINCE opens his briefcase and examines some notes.

GARY: In this scene he takes the kid and...oh God it's making me feel sick! What's the point of it?

VINCE: They call it drama Gary.

GARY: I reckon her head's contaminated.

VINCE: Contaminated?

GARY: Like when animal rights stick dead mice in tins of beans.

VINCE: You can put it down now.

GARY: It's alright, I'm nearly at the end. *(A Beat.)* Wonder what she's like?

TARL: Don't ask that.

GARY: It's alright, I'm nearly at the end.

TARL turns the bargain bucket over. A lone ancient drumstick falls out.

VINCE: I've just spoken to her.

GARY: What did she say?

TARL beholds the drumstick and begins chomping.

VINCE: Wants us to bring her a sandwich and a packet of Monster Munch. Oh shit! Forgot to ask if she's a vegetarian.

GARY: Ring her back.

VINCE: Probably best not to harass her. Do you think she is one?

GARY shrugs.

VINCE: You're not one.

GARY: Doesn't mean she isn't.

VINCE: But it offers an indication.

GARY: Well I don't eat beef.

VINCE: You had a Big Mac on Tuesday.

GARY: I was starving.

VINCE: Better make it cheese and salad.

GARY: Cheese never offended anybody.

VINCE: Unless, she's some sort of raging vegan freak. Sounded like she might be.

GARY: I'll have whatever she doesn't finish.

VINCE: Good man.

VINCE produces a marker pen from his pocket.

VINCE: I'll write this up. Once something's in black and white you always see it more clearly.

During his speech VINCE writes key words on the flipchart like 'HOME SECRETARY', 'WALKABOUT', 'POLEDANCING' and 'FAITHHATE'. GARY stands up, folds his arms and observes.

VINCE: Today the city is playing host to the Home Secretary who is meeting community leaders ahead of next week's council elections. This afternoon he'll be licking brown bottoms at the usual ethnic churches. Then there's an 'all you can eat buffet' at our best curryhouse followed by a top secret trip to a poledancing club where CCTV will be temporarily suspended. The strict security necessitated by the Home Secretary's visit means the rank and file will be on full alert in what's being called Operation Walkabout. Which leaves the crème de la crème, that's you and me Gary, in the fortunate position of taking charge of this station's first official faith hate scenario.

GARY: Brilliant.

VINCE: Operation FaithHate centres on the case of Miss Tar-lo-chan Kaur Grewal, a Sikh playwright whose play is due to open this evening at the Writers' Theatre in Pond Street. A venue famous for championing the dissenting voice in society.

GARY: What does that mean?

VINCE: It puts on plays that nobody wants to see.

GARY: How many officers are assigned to FaithHate Sir?

VINCE: Two. *(A Beat.)* As you've been reading, her script tells the story of...er...

TARL: Don't say it yet.

VINCE: Set in a...a...whatchamacallit...

GARY: Gurdwara AKA Sikh Temple.

TARL: More entertainment!

Suddenly GARY and VINCE, while remaining in character and in the same positions, do a splendid 30 second tap dance to showtime music.

TARL: Stop!

They immediately stop.

TARL: Just spell it out.

VINCE: The subject matter and setting have upset some in the local Sikh community with whom the theatre has been in dialogue over the past month. Leaders of the said community have asked for the script to be changed but the writer has refused to comply, which has made them even more angry. Intelligence suggests we need to be alert to threats to Miss Grewal. And that's where you and me come in Gary. Our objective is to keep her safe and ensure tonight's performance goes smoothly. So, what's your assessment?

GARY: I...er...is it...er...what if this whole situation...

VINCE: Yeah?

GARY: ...is about reptiles manipulating the masses.

VINCE: Eh?

GARY: The illuminati making innocent individuals wage war against each other to keep the people down. They change their faces from lizard to human to lizard to human to confuse you! They're reptilians Sir, controlling over 80 per cent of the world's wealth. Don't you ever wonder where all the missing children are? And what have they done with David Icke?

TARL: Bin all that.

VINCE: A Great British Institution like the Writers' Theatre won't give in to mob rule. I drove past there just now. Saw some Sikh boys hanging about. There was a sense of rage outside and the air felt heavy…with imminent doom. What I don't understand is, why are they so angry?

GARY: Must have their reasons.

VINCE: We can't have angry ethnic minorities telling the rest of us what to do. I reckon you and me have an opportunity today. By protecting Miss Grewal and making sure the show goes on we'll be giving fair play a leg-up. I mean that's the whole point of living in England isn't it?

TARL: This is shit.

GARY and VINCE stop speaking. TARL tears the first page off the flip chart and screws the paper up into a ball. GARY flicks through the script and VINCE ponders on his marker pen.

TARL: Fucking boring crap shit.

Exasperated, TARL throws the ball of paper hard at GARY and VINCE. Again there is no acknowledgement of TARL.

TARL: I need to scare myself.

The Prodigy's 'Firestarter' plays. A stunning young Asian woman, SATINDER, 20s, enters wearing a killer suit and carrying a designer handbag. Like the other characters, SAT does not notice TARL. She speaks out into space though not directly addressing the audience, and skilfully mimes the first action she describes. TARL stares at SAT. Music fades.

SAT: If you take a screwdriver and press the sharp end gently against your left side, you get a little thrill from the tingle of the pain. Go a bit further and you'll draw a drop of blood. Go further and you see proper scarlet. Any more than that and it's agony but then you can't stop and you're so near an organ you think, why not? All the while you know you shouldn't be…but you do it. Because even though it's terrible it's so kind of…

TARL: …beautiful.

SAT: That's what she's doing. To us. In the newsroom, it's just another story. My colleagues don't realise how much harm she's caused because they've never even noticed the people she's hurt. I'm there ticking the diversity boxes to improve my chances. I'm pretending we're all the same and that there's no racism. I'm doing my job, well. Better than the rest of them put together. And then Tarlochan comes along and spoils it, drawing attention to things that are best left unsaid and no-one knows how to place me any more. It's as if I don't belong because she's made our community look like intolerant fools. Because of her, the news editors are starting to doubt me, which isn't fair.

TARL: What else?

SAT: There've been no recorded incidents of anything resembling what she's written. And to set it in our place of worship is obscene. Tarlochan knows exactly what she's doing. She's abused a part of us that goes so deep. You can't understand it unless you are us. She's brought shame on her culture. She is shame. And the public has a right to challenge her.

SAT takes a blackberry out of her handbag and begins to compose an email.

SAT: Once I've got the true facts, I can use my imagination to write the story, just like she does. And I want to know why. Did it really happen? Did it happen to her?

TARL: That's enough.

SAT: I'd like to fuck her up.

TARL: You're not what I thought.

SAT: If she made it up, she's one sick bitch.

TARL: You're a big mistake.

SAT: She's a piece of filth.

TARL: No...no I'm not.

SAT notices GARY and walks around him seductively.

SAT: Maybe me and him can play.

TARL: Don't!

SAT: Imagine the headlines – 'On duty Sikh copper caught in ethnic sex act', 'Ploddy Pantsdown' might work or perhaps just 'Brown Shame'. Bound to be some sort of suspension. Any softly softly reaction would lead to accusations of racial favouritism. God I love the press. We're so...ebony and ivory. His parents might even think I'm a good catch.

TARL: I won't let you pretend what you've made up is real.

SAT: My stories make the truth more bearable.

TARL: Go away. Please.

SAT saunters off the stage. TARL turns her attention back to GARY and VINCE. GARY hurriedly flicks through a file.

GARY: Bloody hell.

VINCE: What?

GARY: She only writes for The bloody Bill! Hey maybe she could get us on, we could show them how it's really done.

VINCE checks his notes.

VINCE: Miss Grewal's currently residing in a flat above the theatre and is adamant she's not moving.

GARY: I don't get it. If it's not safe why's she hanging around?

TARL: I want to watch my play you div. Sorry Gary.

GARY: I don't get it. If it's not safe why's she…

TARL: Maybe you're a bit too divvy.

VINCE and GARY start to pack up and head off.

VINCE: Feels like tonight could be a monumental moment. Humble officers of the law we might be, but we're doing something that actually means something. For our nation.

TARL: Vince doesn't sound right!

They stop.

VINCE: Do you understand what I'm saying?

GARY: Not really Sir.

TARL: You'll have to get rid of him.

VINCE: Better pick up that cheese sandwich, before someone accuses us of religious negligence.

GARY'S phone rings.

GARY: They can't do that!

He answers the phone.

VINCE: I was joking DI Mangat. This is England remember.

GARY comes off the phone.

GARY: I'm afraid you're not coming Sir.

VINCE: What? Who says?

GARY: Orders. I'm going on my own.

VINCE: You? But this is England.

GARY: I can't help that. It's the end of the road.

VINCE: Why?

GARY: There seem to be doubts about your performance. Sorry Sir.

GARY exits.

VINCE: This is outrageous. I'm under orders to deliver a cheese sandwich. And then I've got to… What is it again?

TARL: Operation FaithHate.

VINCE stands alone, crestfallen.

VINCE: But I'm supposed to be the one in charge.

TARL observes VINCE.

TARL: I'm the one in charge.

VINCE: This is going against nature!

TARL: Face it, you're surplus to requirements.

VINCE: Pissing fuck!

VINCE walks off. TARL picks up the red notebook she was writing in and stuffs it in the pocket of her hoodie.

SCENE ONE

Early morning. A banner falls forming a huge backdrop. Painted on it are the words – 'SHAME ON SIKH PLAYWRIGHT FOR HER CORRUPT IMAGINATION'. A gentle-looking elderly man in a turban, MR SIDHU, approaches with AMRIK, a serious-looking dropout to whom life has not been kind. AMRIK is balding and wears a woolly hat and a navy military coat. MR SIDHU wears expensive but mismatched clothes. SIDHU and AMRIK share an approving smile as they regard the banner. As before the characters do not see TARL. A turbanned Sikh youth dressed in black bomber and jeans, KHUSHWANT SINGH BAINS, runs on carrying a black holdall over his shoulder. KHUSH is a bright, sparky thing, filled with too much male energy and a fresh, almost delightful buoyancy. SIDHU warmly pats KHUSH on the back.

SIDHU: *(Pointing to the Banner.)* That's the spirit!

KHUSH indicates AMRIK.

KHUSH: Birji told me what to write.

AMRIK: I gave him the idea, but he put in the hard work.

KHUSH: We'll show those musulmaan…

TARL: …Sulleh's more offensive.

KHUSH: We'll show those sulleh, little bastards coming round college with their Pakistan zindabad chat. They even had these flyers printed saying all shit like you Jat boys go on about defending your religion, what you gonna do about this? Plenty I said. And they're laughing at us, chatting shit like if we got one per cent of this disrespect we'd bomb the heart out of those muthafuckers. We'd bomb the heart out of that whiteman theatre. You lot sit back…

AMRIK: No-one's sitting back.

KHUSH: That's what I said. But the sulleh are so stupid. They don't know how to think, only know how to react. That's why they end up queuing round the block for their dole money.

AMRIK: Need to control your emotions brother.

KHUSH: I even went on the internet to see about making a bomb. I mean I wouldn't have really made one. And even if I had, I wouldn't have used it. But if I could just make one, I'd take it into college to show those sulleh they're not the only lot who can do shit.

SIDHU: We are not concerned with such types of disruption. We are nice, happy folk.

AMRIK: Our niceness is the problem. People think they can say what they like about us.

TARL: Raise the stakes!

AMRIK: If this meeting's our last chance to stop her, how do we play it?

SIDHU: First we tell them we support freedom of speech, as long as the speech is friendly.

AMRIK: Point is we don't operate on a level playing field. I can't go round saying whatever I like about the white institutions because the white institutions won't let me. Tarlochan comes along and the bullshit she spouts about our community intrigues them. They love thinking they're more human than us. Who ever heard of a child...

TARL: Just because no-one's heard, doesn't mean...

SIDHU: Amrik, I am on your side...

TARL: You should be doing something.

The set of a Gurdwara kitchen appears. This comprises a kitchen sink, stainless steel pots and pans, a shelf unit and tea towels.

AMRIK: She's laughing at us and inviting the Goreh theatre people to laugh at us too.

The three characters start washing, wiping and drying the stainless steel utensils and putting them on the shelf unit. This is symbolic of them doing sayva – service in a Gurdwara kitchen.

TARL: All of you working for the benefit of the community. This is good, symbolic.

AMRIK: People who know nothing about Sikhs will start believing her lies. You know what Goreh are like, they only have to start doing Bikram yoga or buy a Madhur Jaffrey cookbook or watch Slumdog Million-fucking-aire and suddenly they're experts on your culture.

SIDHU: Leave the meeting to me. I know how to handle these people.

KHUSH: Have you read it?

AMRIK: Don't need to. They told us the story. Anyway the title says it all. What kind of dickhead writes a play called '*Gund*'?

SIDHU: When I first saw her name on the television – such a beautiful Sikh name – I felt so proud that one of our children was writing for *The Bill*. Happy family entertainment.

AMRIK: Her mum and dad chucked her out.

TARL: Only cos the house got repossessed.

KHUSH: Any girl whose parents don't want to know her isn't worth knowing.

TARL: Dad lost my address when he was pissed.

AMRIK: Gora theatre's her new family.

TARL: Coconut.

AMRIK: How many banners?

KHUSH: Twenty more as big as this. One just says 'Crack the Coconut!'

SIDHU: Even though she is torturing me, I feel pity for her. Why is she doing this nonsense?

TARL: Because…

KHUSH: Because she wants to be a celebrity. So she gets in the papers and on chat shows and all that.

TARL: I'm not good with people.

SIDHU: I've never seen her.

TARL: Don't know how to give them the best of myself.

AMRIK: She avoids the attention on purpose.

TARL: And I smell.

AMRIK: Keeping a low profile makes her seem more interesting than she really is.

TARL: Move on now.

KHUSH gets ready to leave.

KHUSH: Better get the leaflets photocopied. I want them to scatter round that theatre like confetti.

AMRIK: Do the copying there.

KHUSH: They won't let me in.

SIDHU: I'll phone one of my friends at the Council, make sure the theatre's office equipment is available to you.

KHUSH: Thanks Uncleji.

SIDHU: You know our first Gurdwara was a room above a laundry? But we worked hard and gathered our money till we built a palace and put our mark on this city. All the name calling and beating up and laughing at your accent becomes meaningless when you have that mark. Me and your fathers and mothers have been through so much pain. And now this girl, one of our own, hurts us more than we can bear. Doesn't matter whether the Goreh call you Paki or Bin Laden. Their words are nothing compared to the suffering her words are causing.

Suddenly VINCE enters carrying his briefcase and a plastic bag.

VINCE: One ploughman's bap and a packet of Monster Munch.

TARL: What are you doing?

The three Sikh characters behold VINCE, bemused.

VINCE: Thought she might fancy a drink so I got a can of Fanta.

SIDHU: Who are you?

VINCE checks his notes.

VINCE: I'm looking for a Miss Tar-lo-chan Kaur...

AMRIK: *(Interrupts.)* Is this a joke?

VINCE: I assure you I'm a very serious character.

KHUSH: Maybe he's one of the gorah theatre lot!

TARL: Will you please leave!

VINCE: I'm trying to do my job.

SIDHU: You're in the wrong place.

VINCE: I see.

Aggrieved VINCE turns and heads out. AMRIK speaks to KHUSH with the dominance of an officer in command.

AMRIK: How many we expecting from the colleges?

KHUSH: Couple of thousand. Gonna be Khalistani flags waving from all directions. The boys are under orders to rush the building like a sea of soldiers. One phone call from me and it's gonna kick off.

SIDHU: Amrik, remember to keep things calm. We must not spoil our chances at the meeting.

AMRIK: You really think you can talk them round Uncle?

SIDHU'S phone beeps.

SIDHU: Watch and learn from the master!

SIDHU glances at the text he's just received. He tuts in annoyance.

SIDHU: I order nine tandoori chickens, organic! And 20 kilos of meat samoseh, free range! Now they tell me the Home Secretary is a teetotal vegetarian. His people are asking can we make fish samoseh? Where do they think we come from, Bangladesh?

SIDHU exits. KHUSH goes to follow him.

AMRIK: Do your mum and dad know you're here?

KHUSH stops in his tracks.

KHUSH: They don't understand. Don't even go to Gurdwara any more. Too busy sat on the settee eating Pringles and watching X Factor. I hate them.

AMRIK: You know we as a community are our own worst enemies.

KHUSH: How do you mean?

AMRIK: Reading their newspapers, eating their food, sleeping with their women. I tried all that. Learned my lesson. They don't mind us living here but they don't want us taking part. It's easier if you're a woman, like Tarlochan. The Goreh feel sorry for you. If you're a man, you're the oppressor. Truth is they're frightened of us. And jealous. They crave the power our culture gives to our sex. So they're on a mission to emasculate us.

KHUSH: I reckon Khalistan's the answer. A new country back home, just for us.

TARL: *(To AMRIK.)* Say what you want.

AMRIK: I want to be free of all of it.

TARL: And me. Like it never happened. Like she's going to come through that door and play.

41

AMRIK: Free of the suspicion that we stink and beat our wives, free of their preconceived ideas that we work hard at school and we'll take whatever shit they throw at us. We'll tell our own stories in our own theatres, learn our history in our universities, have our own political debates. We're not stupid, we still do business with the Goreh but if we live this way we become stronger. Do you agree brother?

KHUSH: Whatever it takes to honour my religion.

AMRIK: As a leader, your followers will need you to go further than they might themselves. Are you willing to go to any lengths?

KHUSH: I am willing.

TARL produces a gun from her pocket. She points it around the stage.

AMRIK: Today's your chance.

TARL puts the gun in AMRIK'S hand.

TARL: This is for later, you'll know when.

KHUSH: I promise you Birji, we'll stop this play.

AMRIK: It's not enough.

KHUSH: Why?

AMRIK: Because Tarlochan's polluted mind will do it all over again.

TARL holds the gun in AMRIK'S hand and points the weapon at her head.

AMRIK: She's out of control, doesn't care about the damage she's doing. Her thinking is what fuels these Goreh, and that's what needs to be crushed.

KHUSH: I don't understand.

AMRIK: Apparently she can't finish the play.

TARL: I've only just started!

AMRIK: She's written two different endings. Shows she doesn't know what she's doing.

TARL takes the red notebook out of her pocket and flicks through it.

AMRIK: If someone could talk to her and point out the error of her ways, she might change.

KHUSH: That behsharam won't listen to decent folk.

AMRIK: This afternoon she'll be deciding on the ending in the theatre flat. Upstairs from the office where you're copying the leaflets. All you have to do is stay with her till I get there.

KHUSH: But she's got police protection.

AMRIK: My sources say only one officer outside her door. He'll need a piss, eventually. What do you think brother?

KHUSH: I have to be honest Birji, I have got some Goreh mates. And a couple of Kaleh. And one Jewish bloke as well, he's not a close friend, we just sat next to each other in Chemistry and sometimes...he rings me.

AMRIK: You can stay in contact, soon you'll realise they're not friends, they're associates.

KHUSH: And my mum's best mate's called Janet. My dad's is Timothy, Janet's husband.

AMRIK: Your parents are lost, just like Tarlochan.

KHUSH: Didn't realise you knew her so well.

AMRIK: It was in the old days when we made our own theatre. We didn't jump to the Goreh's tune.

KHUSH: What's she like?

AMRIK: Unmemorable, unremarkable. When you find her, you call me, you don't talk to her.

KHUSH: But I want to tell her what I think of her.

AMRIK: There go your emotions again...

KHUSH: Sorry.

AMRIK: You think you can do this? Tell me honestly brother. If not, there are others.

TARL flicks through the red notebook again.

KHUSH: I'll burn her precious play in front of her treacherous eyes!

KHUSH and AMRIK exit. TARL puts the notebook back in her pocket.

SCENE TWO

White sheets on the floor. Solemn Sikh devotional music (singing of Vaheguru) plays low. TARL removes her shoes and covers her head. She walks towards the Guru Granth Sahib – holy book (unseen) and kneels in front of it (placing her forehead on the floor) as is customary in a Gurdwara. A young GIRL wearing a plain beige shalwar kameez enters. The GIRL does not notice TARL but TARL can't take her eyes off her. TARL walks the GIRL towards the book where the GIRL performs the same action as TARL. Holding the GIRL's hand, TARL takes her to sit cross-legged at the side. TARL gently cradles the GIRL in her arms. A young Asian MAN enters and does the same set of actions. The MAN sits down across from the GIRL. The music subsides and the three of them continue the chant of Vaheguru. Moments pass. The MAN and the GIRL stop singing so TARL is left to chant on her own. The MAN stands up and holds his hand out to the GIRL, she takes it and gets up. They go to leave. As TARL watches them both exit, she stops the chant.

SCENE THREE

Morning. Theatre office – a desk, two chairs and a large filing cabinet. Artistic Director of the Writers' Theatre, ANDREW FLEMING, 40s, distant and cool, but easily overwhelmed, enters and sits at the desk. Following him on is Deputy Leader of the Council, JOANNE STEVENSON, also 40s. She's a stout, bullish woman and the smart suit she's dressed in seems to wear her rather than the other way around. Her face is overly made up for the time of day and the flicks in her hair are sprayed to perfection. JOANNE sits opposite ANDREW. Again the characters cannot see TARL who sits at the side.

JOANNE: I'm excited.

ANDREW: Me too.

JOANNE: This whole…atmosphere, it's…compelling. Reminds me of my old university days. I was quite the activist you know.

ANDREW: You?

JOANNE: President of the Student Union! I used to organise all the demos, write the slogans, lead the chanting. Don't think I was ever happier than when I was togged up in my leggings, my DMs and my Free Nelson Mandela sweatshirt. Oh and I had these marvellous CND earrings. They were huge! Bigger than my head. Can't think where they got to. We were all so passionate. God, we believed so hard. Sometimes we'd be marching…this would really piss me off…some nobody on the pavement would shout 'you'll never change anything you bastard students'. I'd yell back 'I'm changing my day you fat fucker!' Apathy, Andrew, is what's killing this country.

ANDREW: I agree.

JOANNE: You know I admire her, but I can't say I'm a fan. If you ask me, the play's a mess. Too many words that don't go together.

ANDREW: Her work is quite stylised.

JOANNE: Can't call a spade a spade can you?

ANDREW: It's heightened.

JOANNE: I do know what stylised means. I'm not a moron.

ANDREW: Of course not.

JOANNE: Don't patronise me Andrew. I'm allowed not to like it.

ANDREW: There is a knack to reading a new play and knowing whether it's good or not.

JOANNE: So you're a better reader than me?

ANDREW: I wouldn't come to the Council offices and question your choices.

JOANNE: Keep your knickers on Andrew, all I'm saying is it's a matter of taste.

ANDREW: It's not, it's really not. It's like understanding a Chablis or cubism.

JOANNE: I don't believe in elitism. I think the achievement of the common man is to be lauded. I'm a great fan of the heroes of reality television. The winners of *Big Brother*, the contestants of *Muslim Driving School* and *Wife Swap*...

ANDREW: Right.

JOANNE: Look, I might not agree with what you say, but I'll defend your right to say it to the death.

ANDREW: Good.

JOANNE: Funny title. 'Gund'.

ANDREW: It's actually pronounced 'Gunddd'. The emphasis is on the D. Means dirt, filth.

JOANNE: Very apt. You know council members were wondering why you'd even entered into this dialogue with the Sikhs.

ANDREW: Given the play's setting, we felt it was inappropriate to put the piece on without informing the local community. I know now that wasn't the smartest move. But I thought they'd be okay…er…perhaps talking to them might even boost our audience figures.

JOANNE: God Andrew, you've no fucking idea.

ANDREW: I was taking my lead from Tarlochan.

JOANNE: I think she wanted to provoke them. She wanted to slap them round the face and for them to take the licks.

ANDREW: You'll have to ask her yourself.

JOANNE: Wish I could go round slapping people round the face. Maybe I will one day.

ANDREW: Her play has far more integrity than you're giving it credit for.

TARL: You're too…static.

JOANNE: Bollocks.

TARL: *(Fast.)* Stand up, sit down, stand up, sit down.

ANDREW and JOANNE stand up and sit down obediently.

JOANNE: We're fighting for her right to shamelessly incite decent citizens.

ANDREW: Thought you were on our side.

JOANNE: I'm here aren't I? The other Councillors wanted me to ask you to postpone the production until after the elections.

ANDREW: I had no idea.

JOANNE: Spineless tossers. You know in my game, it's important to take a stand. People remember you then.

ANDREW: That's exactly what my work at the Writers' Theatre is about. You'll see, tonight is going to be a landmark event in the history of British theatre. People in the industry will realise I'm not afraid of courting controversy. I mean can you imagine if the play causes a riot?

JOANNE: The police will deal with it.

ANDREW: A real riot outside stage door! You don't get much more fucking cutting edge than that Joanne. What we're doing is hugely exciting for this theatre and our city. It's going to put us on the international map.

JOANNE: She's fortunate to have your support.

ANDREW: She's going to be an important writer. Many believe she's got great talent.

JOANNE: Who?

ANDREW: Some of our leading theatre practitioners.

JOANNE: Rich unemployed liberals and depressed homosexuals.

ANDREW: You've just expressed a dangerous prejudice.

JOANNE: Freedom of speech! What I mean is you Oxbridge types are hardly representative of the country.

ANDREW: We're masters of theatre.

JOANNE: I wrote an essay on Wordsworth for my O'levels, doesn't make me a poet. She gets to have her say and carry on doing her job. If politicians offend people we're voted out of office.

ANDREW: So your fate will be decided in the polling stations next week?

JOANNE checks her watch.

JOANNE: Did you tell her I've got to get away for the Home Secretary?

ANDREW: Yes. Look, she's under a great deal of stress.

JOANNE: Is she coming or not?

TARL: No.

JOANNE: By the way, the community leaders have asked to use your office equipment before the rally this afternoon. They want to photocopy some literature.

ANDREW: I don't mind them demonstrating in the lobby but I don't want them swarming into the offices.

JOANNE: It'll show you're trying to be transparent and willing. And the press will love you for it.

JOANNE pointedly checks her watch again.

JOANNE: If she's not going to show, there's no point in me hanging around.

ANDREW: Sorry. But you must understand this is a very difficult time for her.

JOANNE: Does she actually exist?

TARL: What?

JOANNE: I mean she's not just a figment of your imagination?

ANDREW: Don't be ridiculous, you've read the play.

JOANNE: Oh yes Gunddd! A dyslexic mute could have come up with that twaddle.

TARL: You're getting too big for your boots.

JOANNE: Insubstantial doggerel...

TARL: Right!

Suddenly JOANNE falls over clumsily and bangs her head.

ANDREW: Are you okay?

JOANNE: I think so.

He helps her up.

ANDREW: You know I don't think Tarlochan finds it easy to trust. Perhaps she was let down in the past.

JOANNE: Judging by her self-indulgent play, she obviously relies on her ego.

She falls over again.

ANDREW: Honestly Joanne, have you been drinking?

JOANNE: No!

JOANNE reaches for her bag.

JOANNE: Apparently the Home Secretary's shown a real interest in my relationship with the Writers' Theatre. I'll tell him I met her.

ANDREW: Suppose we could be dealing with someone completely different next week, Councillor.

JOANNE: For your sake, I hope it's someone who's sympathetic to the diabolical mess you've made of your finances.

ANDREW and JOANNE go to exit.

ANDREW: Someone like you?

JOANNE: Naturally.

TARL watches them go.

SCENE FOUR

Noon. A camp bed, a door and an old portable television make up the set for the Theatre flat. Crowd sounds from outside. GARY enters gingerly through the door.

GARY: Hello.

TARL: Try to show some initiative.

GARY: Hello...Miss Grewal...

> *GARY immediately checks under the camp bed in SAS fashion. TARL indicates the TV and GARY switches it on. The moving image is projected onto a large screen. ANDREW FLEMING stands on a podium addressing a bustling press conference. TARL and GARY observe.*

ANDREW: We must uphold the right of the artist and ensure that writers have the freedom to express whatever they choose.

> *Loud chanting of 'Off, Off, Off' can be heard in the background.*

ANDREW: We at the Writers' Theatre are proud to present Tarlochan Kaur Grewal's *Gund* – a piece of work that is fearless, provocative and contemporary – everything the Writers' Theatre represents.

JOURNO1: Many local people don't feel they're being listened to. What do you say to those who don't want the play to go on?

ANDREW: Most of them haven't even read it. I believe it's an unrepresentative minority who are objecting to what is clearly an uncompromising satire, packed with dramatic tension and comic...

TARL: Turn it off.

> *GARY turns the television off. He scans the space again and calls out.*

GARY: Miss Grewal?

> *Loud knocking at the door.*

TARL: What's going on?

GARY opens the door to reveal VINCE holding the lunch.

TARL: Oh fucking hell!

VINCE steps into the flat. Again the characters do not notice TARL.

TARL: He's not meant to be here.

GARY: You're not meant to be here.

VINCE: I've got nowhere else to go.

TARL: Should have put you in a uniform Gary, then you could have clubbed him to death with your truncheon.

VINCE: All I know is I'm supposed to deliver this lunch. Feels like I'm in limbo, like I haven't been given a chance.

TARL: Okay stay for a minute while I consider Gary's destiny.

VINCE: Have you had CCTV installed outside the flat?

GARY: Yeah.

VINCE: Been through the hate mail?

GARY: I was just about to.

GARY produces a stack of letters from his pocket.

GARY: *(Opening an envelope.)* Hey someone's sent her a Christmas card!

VINCE: That's nice.

GARY: *(Reads.)* Seasons Greetings. This will be your last Christmas. You are a disgrace to the race. Sending you lots of hate. X.

VINCE: So where is she?

GARY: I think maybe…er…the reptiles have taken her.

TARL: I told you to forget all that!

VINCE: She must be hungry. Maybe if we leave a bit of cheese out she'll show.

GARY: She's not a rodent Sir.

VINCE: If there's no writer then FaithHate is null and void. Fucking hell, there's a tumour forming in my brain Gary! This was supposed to be my big chance.

GARY: I can't help you.

VINCE: Is it because I'm white?

TARL/GARY: No!

The crowd sounds outside get louder.

VINCE: If that many people hated me, I'd kill myself.

TARL/GARY: Oy!

VINCE: Whatever happens I'm sure the show will go on.

GARY: No-one suggested it won't. Did they?

VINCE: Course not. I reckon she's got a right to have her say.

TARLOCHAN turns to GARY.

TARL: What about you?

GARY: I like *The Bill.*

Suddenly there's loud knocking at the door again.

TARL: Fuck.

GARY opens the door and SAT enters. Suited and booted she seems rather demure, exuding a sweet though anxious air.

TARL: Fuck!

SAT: Is she here?

TARL: Get her out!

GARY: Sorry miss but I'm going to have to ask you to leave.

SAT sits down on the camp bed.

SAT: I won't cause any trouble I promise.

TARL drags SAT up from the bed. They struggle. TARL punches her face hard, stunning her. TARL then hurls SAT out of the door. VINCE eyes GARY disdainfully.

VINCE: Do you really think that brown rabble out there will respond to you?

GARY: I don't appreciate that comment!

VINCE: Where is the subject DI Mangat? You can't do your job if she's not here!

TARL: You be quiet!

VINCE: *(Looking around.)* Tar-lo-chan!

VINCE loosens his tie.

VINCE: Tar-lo-chan!

VINCE begins to pant and places his hand on his heart.

GARY: What's happening?

VINCE: I don't feel too good Gary…Gary…

VINCE keels over and reaches out to GARY.

TARL: Leave him.

GARY: Are you alright Sir?

GARY takes his hand.

TARL: I said leave him!

VINCE: I don't want to die.

TARL: Then do what I say.

GARY leads VINCE offstage.

SCENE FIVE

Late morning. White sheets. TARL takes her shoes off, covers her head and goes to pray as before, she then retreats to the side of the stage. A children's version of 'Twinkle Twinkle Little Star' plays. The GIRL enters and goes to sit cross-legged in the middle of the stage. She eats langar (food made in the Gurdwara and presented on a stainless steel thali). The MAN enters and sits next to the GIRL. She carries on eating. He speaks with a strong Punjabi accent.

MAN: Hello Baby.

GIRL: Hello.

MAN: How are you?

GIRL: Very well thank you.

MAN: Ooda, Aada, Eedee… *(The beginning of the Punjabi alphabet.)*

GIRL: A, B, C…

MAN: Ick, Dho, Thin… *(One, two three.)*

GIRL: One, two three…

Suddenly the MAN grabs the girl. It's not clear what he's doing but after a few seconds it's apparent he's tickling her. She laughs hysterically and he laughs with her. She gets away from him and he grabs her again. He tickles her some more and she laughs. This continues until she manages to get away. Then she launches herself at him and starts tickling him. He laughs uproariously. The GIRL cackles and tickles the MAN hard. A comic Hindi version of 'Twinkle Twinkle Little Star' plays.

TARL: This music isn't right.

The music stops. The GIRL and the MAN stop laughing. They come out of character and speak like the actors they are.

GIRL: *(To TARL.)* Is it okay?

TARL recoils, shocked.

TARL: What?

GIRL: The scene, is it okay?

TARL: Er…yeah…

MAN: Good.

TARL watches the GIRL pick up a script.

TARL: I don't…understand…I'm just putting these scenes, your scenes from *Gund* into a new play…you see I'm writing a new play…

Perplexed TARL takes the red notebook out of her pocket and shows them.

GIRL: Have you decided which ending we're doing tonight?

MAN: I mean we've learnt both. Of course.

TARL: Tonight isn't real, I'm just writing…

GIRL: *(Interrupts.)* When will you tell us?

TARL: You're both so vivid. Like you've actually come to life.

MAN: That's down to you.

GIRL: We had some time so we thought we'd go over a few bits.

MAN: Andrew's been so busy with the press.

GIRL: Exciting isn't it?

TARL: So you think this is a real rehearsal?

MAN: *(To GIRL.)* She doesn't like it.

TARL: How come you know I'm here?

GIRL: You're always here.

MAN: You being here helps us to make it more truthful. More real.

TARL: But this…this isn't real.

GIRL: We have to try and make it real don't we? For it to work.

TARL: What?

MAN: Isn't that what you want?

The MAN and the GIRL whisper together.

GIRL: Can we ask you something?

TARL: Yeah.

GIRL: Did it really happen?

TARL: I can't say for sure.

MAN: But the story is based on a real person?

TARL: Yes, I think so.

The GIRL and the MAN exchange an excited look.

GIRL: Who?

TARL: She's dead. I'm positive she's dead.

MAN: So it is real. *(To GIRL.)* Told you. Fancy a coffee?

The GIRL nods and the MAN exits.

TARL: No. No, what's real is something else. That's why I'm writing this new play.

She indicates her red notebook. The GIRL stares at TARL.

GIRL: You must have some idea.

TARL: What?

GIRL: Which ending it is. I mean I need to be clear about my journey.

TARL: In my imagination it's only the first preview.

GIRL: My agent's coming! *(A Beat.)* Is it because of the protest?

TARL: What?

GIRL: Suppose you'll choose the soft option, so you don't offend them any further.

TARL: I don't care about that. It's my play.

GIRL: She's my character, I've shaped her. I created her.

TARL: You didn't.

GIRL: She's mine now.

TARL: Wait, this is stupid...you're nobody. You're just someone I'm making up...

GIRL: I guess we can always go on stage and do whichever ending we like.

TARL: Andrew wouldn't allow it. You'd be sacked...

GIRL: I'm only joking. Don't take everything so seriously. You should learn to let go.

The GIRL heads off. Suddenly the comic 'Twinkle Twinkle' music starts up again. It then stops. Confused, TARL retreats to the side of the stage.

SCENE SIX

Afternoon. Boardroom. ANDREW, JOANNE, SIDHU and AMRIK sit around a huge table. Sounds of the demonstration can be heard outside. In particular there is a loud chant of 'Bole So Nihal'.

AMRIK: No actors are getting through that lot. And if they do they might not feel like acting.

JOANNE: You assured us it would be a peaceful protest.

SIDHU: It is peaceful. They are happy, good boys.

AMRIK: We know the play isn't finished.

ANDREW: A new piece of theatre is always being developed during rehearsals, that's simply the creative process.

AMRIK: Don't fob us off. What's she got planned for the end?

ANDREW: I can't inform you of every minute change to the script. You've already had unprecedented access to Tarlochan's work.

SIDHU: You don't care about our feelings Mr Fleming.

ANDREW: I do care Mr Sidhu. That's why we're here, trying to sort things out. This play is a piece of fiction. It's not real, do you at least accept that?

AMRIK: Our taxes pay for your fictions.

ANDREW: Nothing in *Gund* breaks any law. Look, our theatre empowers artists to explore ideas.

AMRIK: And who decides which artists get to explore these ideas?

ANDREW: Someone's got to do it.

AMRIK: Someone who looks like you, someone who thinks like you think.

ANDREW: There's no need to be personal just because you don't agree with my choices.

AMRIK: Everything you present about us is your take on who we are.

ANDREW: I don't write the plays.

AMRIK: Do you accept that you don't understand us?

ANDREW: No. Dramatic themes are universal. And good writing is good writing wherever it comes from.

SIDHU: I wish someone would write a nice play about a nice subject.

JOANNE: We can't control what people write Mr Sidhu.

SIDHU: Is she keeping it set in the Gurdwara?

ANDREW: Yes.

SIDHU: Please, I'm begging you, ask her to change it to a community centre.

TARL: Wait…

The characters start speaking very quickly.

ANDREW: She is aware of your views but she will not compromise the setting.

AMRIK: So what are you going to do?

ANDREW: We hope to go ahead as planned.

AMRIK: Are you prepared to delay the opening?

ANDREW: No.

AMRIK: What's the point of this meeting if you're not going to listen?

TARL: Slow down…

ANDREW: You are being listened to.

JOANNE: I for one am listening.

SIDHU: You have to make some concessions.

ANDREW: We're discussing those issues now.

AMRIK: Tarlochan should be here.

TARL: No, I don't want to…

JOANNE: He does have a point.

ANDREW: It's not appropriate.

TARL: I don't have to be in it.

SIDHU: We can't have this meeting without her!

The dialogue reaches a crescendo.

AMRIK: *(Shouts.)* This is rubbish.

TARL approaches.

AMRIK: All these words, they're rubbish!

TARL: No they're not.

AMRIK: War! This is war.

TARL: *(Shouts.)* No it's not.

The characters stand up and look at TARL, she recoils in shock.

ANDREW: Tarlochan, what are you doing here?

TARL: What?

SIDHU: So this is the girl?

JOANNE: At last!

AMRIK: Long time no see.

TARL: This is wrong.

SIDHU: She's much shabbier than I expected.

JOANNE: So you do exist!

TARL: No…I'm…I'm not in it.

ANDREW: In what?

TARL: I don't know how to be.

ANDREW: Your being here isn't a good idea.

TARL: I know, but this isn't right, you're not saying my words.

The characters look at each other, confused.

JOANNE: What's she on about now?

ANDREW: Best if you come back later.

AMRIK: You look like shit. What happened to you?

TARL: I'm not sure what's going on.

SIDHU: Brain damage.

ANDREW: This is a very stressful time for her.

Frozen to the spot, TARL stares at the characters.

TARL: *(Urgent.)* Stand up, sit down, stand up, sit down...

Nothing happens.

TARL: Stand up, sit down...

ANDREW: What are you saying Tarlochan?

TARL: Stop this now!

ANDREW: I'm sorry but you're going to have to wait outside.

TARL: Outside? Where?

ANDREW: In the corridor.

SIDHU: Please I beg you change it to a community centre.

TARL: What?

SIDHU: Why are you torturing us?

TARL: I don't understand.

AMRIK: She won't talk to you Uncle.

JOANNE: Can we please get on?

The characters sit back down.

ANDREW: Look it's my right to support this writer and to produce her work.

SIDHU: Having the right does not mean it is right. The point is that this young lady is a bad apple.

Stunned TARL observes the characters as the scene continues.

ANDREW: She's an artist, she's going to offend some people. Surely?

SIDHU: So you admit it is offensive! *(A Beat.)* How long have you lived in this city Mr Fleming?

ANDREW: Sixteen months.

SIDHU: I have resided here for nearly forty years. This is my home. And to have such pain inflicted on me in my own home is wrong.

AMRIK: We're the lifeblood of this city, it's us you should be entertaining. Why can't I bring my mum and dad and mates into this building to see a show that means something to us?

ANDREW: You can.

AMRIK: You don't want to include us. This time we're not having it, that's what you can't stand.

ANDREW: I admit we need to do better. That's why I'm trying to include you now.

AMRIK: You don't know how to relate to people like me.

ANDREW: Plenty of my staff come from different ethnic backgrounds.

AMRIK: None of them make decisions though and the ones who challenge you always end up leaving.

SIDHU: Please Mr Fleming, realise you are going too far.

ANDREW: Tarlochan is exploring sensitive issues and yes the play might shock some people. That ability to challenge, coupled with decent writing is what constitutes great theatre. And if you don't understand that simple principle...

SIDHU: You think I'm thick!

JOANNE: Let's all calm down.

TARL: Please...this is going wrong...

JOANNE: Will you stop butting in?

ANDREW: I really think you should wait outside.

TARL: Yes, okay. Maybe I'll go and come back...and then things'll be back to normal.

ANDREW: Whatever makes you feel comfortable.

Perplexed TARL half nods. The characters watch her exit.

AMRIK: We are also here to protect Tarlochan. She's still one of us and we've heard certain things.

ANDREW: What things?

SIDHU: Sadly there are a few hotheads amongst our number who are not satisfied by talking.

JOANNE: Then you must deal with them.

AMRIK: Thought you cared about her.

ANDREW'S phone rings. He checks the screen.

ANDREW: I'll be back.

AMRIK: Who's left Mr Fleming?

ANDREW: What?

AMRIK: To care about her.

ANDREW exits.

JOANNE: Would anyone like some tea?

SIDHU: No tea.

AMRIK: So what now Joanne?

SIDHU: You think I have fought this hard to make my home here that I will stop fighting just because of what that man says.

JOANNE: What do you mean by fighting?

AMRIK: What do you mean by it?

JOANNE doesn't respond.

AMRIK: With modern communications, ordinary people have the power to become generals of their own armies. Anyone anywhere could receive a call to arms.

JOANNE: That kind of talk might get Andrew all hot and bothered but I'm afraid it doesn't faze me.

SIDHU: All Amrik means is that systems are in place.

AMRIK's phone rings. He takes the call and goes to the side.

SIDHU: You know Joanne I think you are a nice lady.

JOANNE: Thank you.

SIDHU: I have always supported you and I have always urged the residents of your ward to support you. What I have done is like asking people to keep buying the same washing powder, even though there is another cheaper, better washing powder on the shelf. Do you know why I ask them?

JOANNE: Because we share common principles.

SIDHU: No. Because we have an understanding.

JOANNE: Mr Sidhu…

SIDHU: An unspoken, indefinable understanding. Like it is always in the air. Like it is air. How can you expect people to buy a washing powder which stains their clothes?

JOANNE: Mr Sidhu, I think we should keep artistic matters separate from community matters.

SIDHU: That is the exact problem, they have been kept separate. Artistic issues must be monitored, otherwise people can go round making things up.

AMRIK comes off the phone.

AMRIK: Word on the street is the Home Secretary doesn't want his thunder stolen by some stupid play.

JOANNE: The police will ensure things remain calm.

AMRIK: They can't cope with my boys. I reckon the opening will be delayed. Give us time to negotiate, get mobilised.

JOANNE: That isn't going to happen. *(A Beat.)* I can see how passionately you both feel but I won't budge. The play's going on without any changes, and that's final.

AMRIK: No-one's listening to us Joanne.

JOANNE: I am. Let the play happen and you will be perceived as the dignified, tolerant community the country knows you to be. By getting all fired up you're giving Tarlochan and her work even more publicity.

AMRIK: *(To SIDHU.)* She's trying to manipulate you.

JOANNE: I don't believe for one minute she's this brilliant writer. If this *Gund* play is shown, people will see the flaws in the writing and her own work will expose her as the mediocre artist she really is. So in a funny way, you'll be proved right. But to stop her having her say, just isn't possible.

SIDHU: What about our say?

JOANNE: I've been thinking about that. If you write a statement outlining your grievances, I'll make sure the theatre manager reads it out at the start of the play. You'll have a captive audience, taking in your words before they listen to her words. You, the real people will be the voice of reason while the luvvies indulge themselves in her pretentious crap!

SIDHU: I could write something.

AMRIK: It's a token gesture.

SIDHU: I'll teach that girl how to use proper English grammar!

ANDREW comes back in, he's visibly agitated and approaches AMRIK.

ANDREW: Your demonstrators have been threatening my box office staff.

AMRIK: Maybe your customer service isn't up to scratch.

ANDREW: Those workers just about earn the minimum wage. None of this is their fault.

TARL enters and marches up to the middle of the stage.

SIDHU: You should pay your staff more.

ANDREW: I want you out.

TARL: No! Ask them to stay, they're supposed to stay!

Nothing happens. All the characters watch TARL who is becoming increasingly distressed.

ANDREW: Did the police forget your lunch?

TARL: Why aren't you saying what I'm writing?

SIDHU: I told you, she has brain problems.

A fraught TARL goes up to AMRIK and takes the gun out of his pocket.

JOANNE: Shouldn't the police be with her?

TARL assumes a shooting position.

JOANNE: Oh my God.

The characters leap to their feet and shout and scream in fear. ANDREW'S arms fly up in surrender. MR SIDHU immediately lies on the floor face down. TARL fires the gun at the characters but only a few sorry clicks sound. In despair, TARL drops the gun. AMRIK quickly retrieves it. The characters breathe a collective sigh of relief. ANDREW angrily turns to TARL.

ANDREW: Have you lost your mind?

TARL: I was just trying something.

ANDREW: *(To AMRIK.)* How dare you bring a firearm into my building.

AMRIK: I didn't even know it was there. She must have planted it on me.

They all turn to look at TARL.

TARL: It's only a pretend one, you can check.

AMRIK checks it and nods.

JOANNE: That was not funny young lady!

SIDHU: We could press charges.

ANDREW: She didn't mean anything by it, did you Tarlochan?

TARL: No.

ANDREW: She's under a great deal of pressure.

AMRIK: Things are going to get a lot worse.

ANDREW: Will you please leave?

SIDHU: Mark my words, this story is not finished yet!

AMRIK and SIDHU head out. A shocked ANDREW turns to TARL.

ANDREW: What the hell were you thinking?

TARL: I don't know.

JOANNE: We can hardly accuse them of intimidating behaviour while you're trying to murder us all.

ANDREW: Quite.

TARL: Sorry.

ANDREW: Anyway, we're fucked.

ANDREW sits down and rubs his eyes. He downs a jug of water.

ANDREW: The police have asked me to delay the opening by an hour.

TARL: No!

JOANNE: *(Shocked.)* What?

ANDREW: They're totally outnumbered, most of their officers are protecting your bloody man.

JOANNE: This is unbelievable.

ANDREW: They can't ensure the safety of the actors. I've no choice. You've got to convince these people Joanne.

JOANNE: They think they can bully me, after everything I've done for them. Well they bloody well can't. *(A Beat.)* The Sikhs have asked to read out a statement before the performance.

TARL: But that's giving in.

ANDREW: Might it shut them up?

JOANNE: Be like cutting their tongues out.

TARL: No-one wants to listen to some diatribe, not in the theatre, not at the start of a show.

ANDREW: I'm prepared to do whatever it takes to get your work on. Besides nobody ever remembers the beginning, it's all about the end, eh Tarlochan?

JOANNE: Is there any tea going?

ANDREW: I'll find someone to bring it up.

JOANNE: You make it.

ANDREW: I don't know how to work the urn.

JOANNE: You must have been camping as a boy.

TARL: Is the play still happening?

ANDREW: Of course.

JOANNE: Of course.

ANDREW: We're going up late that's all.

ANDREW'S phone rings. He turns it off and starts to head out.

ANDREW: *(To TARL.)* By the way the atmosphere outside is playing havoc with the actors' mental health.

TARL stares at him.

ANDREW: They're losing their focus in the onion scene. Can you come into the studio and offer some moral support?

TARL nods blankly. A shaken TARL watches ANDREW exit.

JOANNE: Try not to worry about the demonstration.

TARL: Am I still me?

JOANNE: Must be hard, I mean for your life to be threatened...

TARL: ...or am I writing me?

JOANNE: Rest assured that you have the Council's unequivocal support. I know how you must be feeling. As a woman in politics one is constantly doing battle. One needs tenacity, self-belief, stamina.

TARL: Is my play still happening?

JOANNE: No question. Don't worry about your friendly neighbourhood Sikhs, they'll do as they're told. I mean why shouldn't you attack what's wrong with your culture...

TARL: There's nothing wrong with my culture. No more than with yours.

JOANNE: I blame the parents. Parents across cultures. Do you know that poem? *(She quotes the first stanza of 'This Be The Verse' by Philip Larkin.)*

TARL: Yes!

JOANNE: What about your family?

TARL: The police are supposed to bring me a sandwich and some crisps.

JOANNE: Well these days your friends are your family.

TARL: There's nobody.

JOANNE: You've caused a proper rumpus with your play.

TARL: I wanted to say something.

JOANNE: Oh very fancy!

TARL: If you make people feel, then they might start thinking.

JOANNE: I think we all think too much.

TARL: And I always felt like planting a bomb.

JOANNE: Andrew said you encouraged his discussions with the Sikhs

TARL: Maybe I hoped there might be some brown faces in the audience.

JOANNE: You got that one wrong, they're all outside the building. I left my career for politics because I care about people and I want a better society.

TARL: You should have stayed in teaching.

JOANNE: How do you know I was a teacher?

TARL: You look like a drunk with a job.

JOANNE: Are you bipolar?

TARL: Things just sort of come out of me.

JOANNE: There are people outside who want you dead because of what comes out of you.

TARL: I wanted my words to go into their heads. I won't pretend they don't exist. I am of them. And they are of me.

JOANNE: You've lost me now.

TARL: It's not my job to be sensitive and considerate. I hate the quiet softness and tranquillity that people yearn for.

JOANNE: There's a terrible sense of unease about you. Disease. Like Disease.

Sound of police sirens.

TARL: That might be my lunch.

JOANNE: You have my word Tarlochan, I'll fight for you and your play with every breath in my body.

TARL: I'll pray that you keep breathing then.

JOANNE: Just when you thought things couldn't get any weirder!

SCENE SEVEN

Afternoon. White sheets on the floor. TARL approaches and takes her shoes off and covers her head. She goes to pray. The actor playing the GIRL enters.

GIRL: Are you showing me because I'm not doing it properly?

TARL: No…no…you're…perfect.

GIRL: Thanks.

TARL: Are you alright?

GIRL: What?

TARL takes her hand. The GIRL moves away awkwardly. The MAN enters.

GIRL: I'd better get on.

TARL watches as the actors playing the GIRL and the MAN go through the blocking on the set for the next scene they are rehearsing. This includes a stainless steel kitchen unit (same as the one from Scene One), stainless steel cooking utensils, tins of food, bags of onions and packets of flour.

VINCE: Tar-lo-chan!

VINCE waves from the side.

VINCE: Got your Ploughmans!

TARL joins him and blankly starts to chomp on the sandwich from his plastic bag. VINCE holds out a packet of Monster Munch into which she delves ravenously. He grins as he watches the actors.

VINCE: So this is showbusiness!

He eyes her as she takes a bite, it's not pretty.

VINCE: Looks like you're enjoying that.

VINCE gestures towards a window.

VINCE: That lot outside, they're not like us. Don't think the same, don't have the same values. I've said it before, you can't reason with terrorists...

The comic 'Twinkle Twinkle' plays and then stops suddenly.

TARL: *(To VINCE.)* Did you hear that music?

VINCE: Afraid not, the job's stifled most of my creativity.

He nods to the window again.

VINCE: The uniforms out there are a bunch of kids. All the big boys are with the Home Secretary.

TARL: You could have a word with them.

VINCE: We're all different departments, if you speak out of turn health and safety'll come round and make you do ashtanga yoga for six months.

VINCE receives a text. He indicates his phone.

VINCE: He's only gone and locked himself in the Gents! To think the powers that be believed Gary could handle FaithHate on his todd!

He goes to leave.

VINCE: Feels like I'm living the white man's burden all over again. Chin up eh Tar-lo-chan?

He exits. TARL watches as the actors start the scene. The GIRL and the MAN start stacking various items onto the kitchen unit.

MAN: You my friend?

GIRL: Might be.

The MAN lifts up a pot which the GIRL has put on the wrong shelf.

MAN: This one go here Baby.

She giggles.

MAN: Why you laughing?

She giggles uncontrollably and doubles up, almost in pain from the laughter.

GIRL: You talk...you talk like a proper Paki.

MAN: Shut up.

GIRL: *(Imitating him.)* Shut up.

MAN: You a Paki, just like me.

The GIRL stops laughing.

GIRL: No I'm not.

She picks up an onion and sniffs it hard.

GIRL: That's what you smell like.

She pushes the onion into the man's nose.

GIRL: You should have baths.

MAN: I do.

GIRL: I know you don't.

MAN: I have bath.

GIRL: Bathsss you idiot. Bathsss. Make sure you learn English properly before you come and get me from school. And don't show up outside the gates with your smelly Paki friends. You're so stinking well embarrassing.

Suddenly the GIRL comes out of character.

GIRL: Sorry...I've lost it...

ANDREW hops onto the set. The GIRL is quite upset.

GIRL: I don't know what I'm doing any more.

ANDREW: It's okay.

TARL: You don't mean it.

ANDREW: I think she does.

GIRL: How can I play this moment if I don't know how it ends?

ANDREW: She's simply being a child – naughty, precocious, provocative.

TARL: It's not your fault.

ANDREW: *(To the GIRL.)* Less thinking and more being!

ANDREW walks the GIRL round the unit.

ANDREW: So you put a couple of tins onto the shelf, then the pot goes here, laugh…ha ha ha…and say the lines. Then as you take the onion, push it right into his face!

MAN: You never used to be that aggressive.

GIRL: She's a strong character, she has to be forceful.

MAN: Surely the aggression's in the lines?

ANDREW: I like it.

GIRL: For God's sake we're supposed to be opening tonight, which ending is it?

TARL: I'm not sure, you see I've been working on something else.

GIRL/MAN: What?

ANDREW: Tarlochan! You have a duty to the artistic team to make a decision! To finish *Gund*!

GIRL: Do I live or die?

TARL starts walking around the stage manically.

ANDREW: *(To TARL.)* Why don't you go and sit in the Green Room? Have a biscuit.

TARL is running now. She's hitting the scenery, trying to break it down, desperately looking for a way out.

ANDREW: What the hell are you doing?

TARL: Must be a way out somewhere.

ANDREW: *(To the actors.)* Okay, take five.

The puzzled actors exit. TARL follows them out but quickly comes back in.

TARL: Everywhere's just white space.

TARL pummels the flats at the back but can find no exit. She collapses in a heap. The comic 'Twinkle Twinkle' music starts to play. It then stops. TARL tries to compose herself.

TARL: The Twinkle Twinkle music at the end of the first scene, it's not right.

ANDREW: But you suggested it.

TARL: Did I?

ANDREW: In the stage directions.

TARL: I've changed my mind.

ANDREW: You can't keep exerting control like this. Have faith in my interpretation.

TARL springs up.

TARL: We have to do the play!

ANDREW: As soon as the police give the all clear. Anyway the rest of the cast aren't even here, they've been blockaded inside Starbucks.

TARL: Lets perform it in there.

ANDREW: It's not safe for you to leave the theatre.

TARL: That's up to me.

ANDREW: This doesn't just affect you Tarlochan, I have to consider my staff, the actors, the building…

TARL: Please…

ANDREW: *(Irritated.)* Can you for one second think about someone other than yourself? I had other plays I could have programmed you know, some of which had endings! If you hadn't agreed to this dialogue in the first place, we might not be in this mess.

TARL: If my play was on and just your usual blue rinse brigade were seeing it, so what? Nothing would change.

ANDREW: So it's change you're after?

TARL: I've got a right…

ANDREW: Yes.

TARL: If I haven't then I might as well stop breathing.

ANDREW: You must be frightened.

TARL: No I'm desperate. I've waited for this my whole life… And I'm scared if it doesn't happen soon, I'll lose my chance.

ANDREW: If it helps we're in the same boat. I've ploughed a large chunk of the theatre's marketing budget into this production. My reputation's on the line.

TARL: You're certain this is only a delay?

ANDREW: You have to trust me. Oh, I ought to mention… there's been more talk of threats, people wanting you hospitalised and so forth. They seem to hold you personally responsible.

TARL: I am.

ANDREW: I have to make sure that you're aware.

The actors walk back on. TARL retreats to the side with ANDREW.
The GIRL and the MAN position themselves on the set.

ANDREW: *(To the actors.)* Okay, go from Baths.

GIRL: Bathsss you idiot. Bathsss. Make sure you learn English properly before you come and get me from school. And don't show up outside the gates with your smelly Paki friends. You're so stinking well embarrassing.

They stare at each other.

GIRL: Do you understand Paki? You'd just better do what I say.

Suddenly the MAN grabs the GIRL and holds her upside down by the ankles. She half laughs and half cries. He shakes her hard and releases her. She falls with a thud onto the floor.

GIRL: I'm telling.

She tries to run past the MAN but he blocks her. She turns and runs, the MAN speeds after her and catches her.

TARL: Tell him to stop!

ANDREW: What?

TARL rushes onto the set.

TARL: Stop, leave her alone!

She hurriedly pulls the MAN off the GIRL. The actors jump up defensively.

MAN: What the fuck!

ANDREW: They're trying to play the scene!

TARL: Where are their scripts?

The actors drift off.

ANDREW: They've been off the book for weeks!

TARL: Oh yes…yes…Sorry…I'm sorry.

Loud sounds of chanting from outside.

ANDREW: Tarlochan, hadn't you better decide on the ending?

He indicates a fat script.

TARL: Yes. Yes, you're right. I must.

She sits down at the desk and opens the script, she starts to write. The GIRL comes back on and starts re-stacking the kitchen unit. ANDREW approaches the GIRL.

ANDREW: At some point during rehearsals the writer always becomes surplus to requirements.

TARL stops writing and closes the fat script.

SCENE EIGHT

Late afternoon. KHUSH stands at the photocopier. Hundreds of leaflets are piled high by the machine. TARL enters and watches him do the copying. KHUSH is immediately anxious.

KHUSH: Afternoon. I've got permission. *(Hands her a leaflet.)* Have one.

TARL: *(Reads.)* Don't let the white racist theatre abuse your heritage. Have pride in your religion. Stop Tarlochan Kaur Grewal from spreading her evil lies…

KHUSH: You one of them who work here? *(A Beat.)* You look like one of us.

TARL: I'm her.

KHUSH moves away, disturbed.

KHUSH: You? You're not.

TARL: Why?

KHUSH: Thought you'd have better clothes. Thought you'd look more like a Goree.

TARL: Say your name.

KHUSH: Khush.

TARL: Happy.

KHUSH: I hate you.

TARL: But we've only just met. Properly.

TARL composes herself and takes the fat Gund *script out of her pocket.*

TARL: Is this what you want, *Gund?*

KHUSH: Come on then, let's have a look.

They walk around the space as though they're playing cat and mouse. TARL shoves the script up her sweatshirt and folds her arms.

KHUSH: *(Shouts.)* You make me sick! I fucking hate you!

TARL approaches him and takes his hand.

TARL: Thank you, Happy.

KHUSH: What?

TARL: For teaching me tolerance. I love you. The most out of all of them.

He pushes her away.

KHUSH: I'm nothing to do with you. Why do you hate your own community so much?

TARL: I'm only a writer.

KHUSH: Then you should write about things in a helpful way.

TARL: I was trying my best.

KHUSH: It's not fair. All those poor people who have to be in hospital and you're walking around free using your arms and legs and your sick brain. *(Quiet.)* Behsharam... kuthee... *(Shameless bitch.).*

TARLOCHAN freezes.

TARL: What did you call me?

KHUSH: You heard.

> *TARL suddenly grabs KHUSH'S ear. He falls over and screams in pain.*

TARL: You're not my mum or my dad. You don't know me or what goes on in my head. You boys. Getting sent to private school, as if that's going to kickstart your woolly brains. Being spoilt with Nintendo and fat trainers and microwave chips.

> *She lets him go. He gets his breath back and stands up.*

KHUSH: All the girls I know hate you too. And the old ladies and the middle-aged ones as well.

TARL: None of my business what anyone thinks. Whatever I've done is between me and God.

KHUSH: No way is my God your God.

TARL: Where's your God then? In your beard or under your turban?

KHUSH: You don't believe what I believe.

> *TARL takes off her shoes, pulls her sweatshirt over her head and puts her hands together.*

TARL: Ek umkar, satnam, karta purkh *(One god, named truth, creator.)*...

KHUSH: Stop.

> *TARL continues. KHUSH cups his hands over her mouth. She carries on praying.*

KHUSH: I don't want to hear those words coming out of your mouth.

> *TARL breaks free.*

TARL: I want to say them, I need to say them.

They tussle again. TARL falls to the ground.

KHUSH: You're doing this to aggravate me.

TARL: No. Because I have to...

Shattered, they sit on the floor and face each other.

TARL: I'm saying it in my head.

KHUSH: Shut up.

TARL: What are you going to do, crack it open?

KHUSH: I wish you were dead.

TARL: That's a kind religious thought.

KHUSH: My words and actions are the result of your words and actions.

TARL: Don't remind me Happy! *(A Beat.)* If you don't want to hear me saying it, you say it, pray for my bad soul.

KHUSH: Why do you want to crush our people?

TARL: Just because we've been through shit, doesn't mean we don't make our own shit.

KHUSH: It's cos you want to be a goree.

TARL: Where do you see me being that?

KHUSH: You just are.

She gets up.

TARL: Your mum and dad have got a shop haven't they?

KHUSH: How do you know?

TARL: They sell beefburgers. And Marlboro lights.

KHUSH: Those two are nothing to do with me.

TARL: So which people are you fighting for?

KHUSH: My principles.

TARL: Is your faith so weak?

KHUSH: Shut up, you're the enemy within.

TARL: Your head's got all mixed up.

KHUSH: How could it not be living in this shithole?

TARL: But you've got a nice shop.

KHUSH: I mean England.

TARL: You want to nick some notes out of the till and buy one of them round the world tickets. Stick a rucksack on your back and see a bit of life.

KHUSH: I'm going home back to the Punjab. Gonna be a farmer, drive a tractor and work the land, our real proper land.

TARL: Like it out there do you?

KHUSH: *(A Beat.)* I've never been.

TARL: *(Laughs.)* You won't last five minutes.

KHUSH: I'll be with my brothers and sisters.

TARL: They're all getting visas to come here.

KHUSH: I'll find people there who want to practise my religion with their hearts full of the love of God. I'm sick of the hypocrites here. Like my mum and dad, who go round buying half a ton of gold for the wedding of some nobody they've never met. Get dressed up like a pair of Bollywood pimps and sit in the Gurdwara wishing the time away till they can get merry. I hate it when they bring the book, our holy book, to some three star hotel where men are dancing with bottles of Johnny Walker on their heads.

TARL: I used to hate all that.

KHUSH: No-one's bothered. Everyone just wants and wants and wants.

TARL: They can't help it, their souls have been infected. You know you should come and see *Gund...*

KHUSH: Never. You're worse than all of them, you've gone somewhere you'll never come back from.

TARL: Do you reckon that lot out there are like you?

KHUSH: Yeah.

TARL: Those boys couldn't care less. They're here to feel the beats of the dhol, tell off a behsharam like me and get high on the party atmosphere.

KHUSH: There are women outside as well.

TARL: Someone has to keep you alive. You're just as different from them as I am. You're the one that's most like me.

KHUSH: Fuck off.

TARL: How are you getting on with Amrik?

KHUSH: He's like my older brother.

TARL: Amrik's an atheist, he got put off at an early age.

KHUSH: You're a liar.

TARL: When Amrik was a boy, his mum used to send him to learn Gurmukhi at the Gurdwara. But he got confused by the lamah so the Gianis beat him. One day one of them stuck a hot iron on his hand, left a dark red mark. Have you seen it?

KHUSH shakes his head.

TARL: Take a look sometime. He called it his warrior mark. If anyone asked him about it, he'd say 'Got into a fight with a pig at a demo'.

KHUSH: Shut up.

TARL: Aren't you supposed to tell him you've got me?

KHUSH quickly searches for his phone.

TARL: Why do you believe so hard?

KHUSH: I just do.

TARL: Perhaps because there's not much else going on.

Fury consumes KHUSH.

KHUSH: You're no Sikh, you fake. No-one gives a shit about you or your pretend faith. Give me that piece of shit you call a script and I'll burn it. I'll burn this whole motherfucking theatre down.

Suddenly TARLOCHAN throws him the Gund script which he catches. She turns to go.

TARL: Go on then brother. Light up.

KHUSH attempts to stop her, TARL brushes him off.

TARL: Don't get your kuchee in a twist.

KHUSH: You don't know what I'm gonna do.

TARL: I'm pretending to be a brave Sikh, like you are.

KHUSH: I'm telling you I'm setting it on fire!

He takes out a lighter. TARL continues out.

TARL: If it's still here when I get back, we'll both know there's a God.

She exits.

SCENE NINE

The GIRL sits on a wooden stool in front of the stainless steel kitchen unit. Her hands and feet are tied up with pieces from a white sheet. She's only wearing her vest and pants and her shalwar kameez lies in a pile on the floor. The MAN stands next to her, he's tearing up a white sheet.

GIRL: *(Screams.)* Help!

MAN: No-one can hear you Baby.

GIRL: Sorry for what I said.

MAN: Sure?

GIRL: I'm just a stupid little girl. I'm sorry, I'm sorry, I'm sorry…

MAN: Too late.

The MAN opens a packet of flour and throws it over the GIRL. She starts to cry.

GIRL: I'm telling my dad. Everything.

MAN: I told him already. He's coming to see you now.

The MAN takes one of the strips he's torn from the white sheet and gags the GIRL with it.

MAN: Can't hear you Baby, talk louder.

Muffled sounds from the GIRL's mouth. The MAN pulls the gag even tighter. The GIRL is extremely distressed.

MAN: Come on Baby, talk louder. Louder!

SCENE TEN

Early evening. The Stage. The GIRL remains gagged on the stool, she is dimly lit. Loud sounds of chanting and unrest can be heard from outside. (VINCE/GARY/TARL and AMRIK/SIDHU/JOANNE do not acknowledge one another or the GIRL as their respective dialogue proceeds.) MR SIDHU is sitting down, writing on a piece of paper. He looks up.

SIDHU: Just because this girl has a Sikh name does not mean she is a Sikh…I for one have never seen her at the Gurdwara…

VINCE and GARY enter running towards a neon Ladies sign. They stop.

VINCE: *(Shouts.)* Tar-lo-chan! Did you confiscate her belt and shoelaces?

GARY: She's not the type to top herself.

VINCE: That rabble have got to her.

GARY: Don't suppose you've ever considered why they're so angry?

VINCE: Tar-lo-chan, we're the bearers of glad tidings!

GARY: I'm asking you to listen.

VINCE: That is exactly why the Great's gone out of Great Britain. Every asylum seeking economic illegal migrant thinks he's got the right to have his say. Whatever happened to keeping quiet and suffering?

A triumphant AMRIK enters. SIDHU gets up.

SIDHU: The statement is complete!

AMRIK: Who cares about that? My boys have ringfenced the theatre. They won't rest till they've brought this city to its knees!

SIDHU: I don't want to pick up the pieces of your mess.

AMRIK receives a text.

AMRIK: My mess will bring about the result you can't. Maybe if you and your lot had fought harder we wouldn't be here.

He glances at his phone.

AMRIK: Khush has got the girl.

SIDHU: Our aim is to stop the play, we are not kidnappers.

AMRIK: You wait, she'll tell the press she got it all wrong. Then she'll thank me for making her see sense.

SIDHU: You will set the whole community back.

AMRIK: Isn't that your favourite bit? After the mayhem on the streets...it's over to you, having Marks and Spencer sandwiches with the councillors and the cops. All of you going on about how bad it is and how you'll make the peace. And you do, in your elastoplast way until the next time, and then you go back for more sandwiches.

SIDHU: Why are you talking like this?

AMRIK: You're partly to blame for the way the goreh portray us, you make them feel as if they know us.

SIDHU: You think influence comes without sacrifice? The goreh like me, they listen to me...

AMRIK: Our people have changed. They want to listen to a new song.

SIDHU: We have Sikhism.

AMRIK: Come on Uncle, if you were a man of God, you'd let her have her say.

SIDHU: You disrespect me just like she disrespects me.

GARY: *(To VINCE.)* You don't know anything about me or my culture. I might as well be a white bloke.

VINCE: That's what you want isn't it? To be accepted like everyone else.

GARY: We can't have a conversation without you knowing best or taking the piss.

VINCE: I am in charge DI Mangat.

GARY: You came back and took over.

VINCE: This is how it's supposed to be. In England.

AMRIK: Why did you bring us to this fucking country?

SIDHU: For a better life.

AMRIK: Well here we are.

AMRIK goes to leave.

SIDHU: Amrik!

AMRIK ignores him and exits. TARL emerges from the Exit sign.

VINCE: You're alive Tar-lo-chan! Brilliant.

VINCE'S phone rings, he goes to the side to answer it.

GARY: Starbucks has been liberated. The actors are out.

TARL: So the play's on?

GARY: Yeah.

VINCE comes off the phone. Agitated JOANNE runs on.

VINCE: Some woman's waiting for you in the foyer. A Miss Satinder Shergill.

TARL: The journalist?

VINCE: From the *Mail,* yeah.

TARL: I can't meet her.

VINCE: I've taken the call now. You have to go.

TARL: But you're supposed to keep me safe.

The GIRL's dead body falls from the stool.

VINCE: Don't worry, Gary's going to escort you.

GARY starts dragging TARL offstage.

JOANNE: *(To SIDHU.)* The police are having to bring officers in from the neighbouring constabulary!

SIDHU: You must stop this play.

JOANNE: I can't. Look, your grievances have been aired to a national audience, it's time to call the protest off.

SIDHU: What did the Home Secretary's people say?

JOANNE: Please Mr Sidhu…

SIDHU: If this play goes on blood will be shed.

JOANNE: I've been thinking, the next time there's the slightest whiff of offensive material we'll come down on them like a sledgehammer to a brittle bone.

SIDHU: The police cannot cope and the Home Secretary will not set the army on civilians because of the bloody theatre. You are going to end up with no play and a nightmare in our city. You have created this Joanne, so it's up to you to use your imagination and find a way out.

TARL: No...please...I don't want to see her.

VINCE: We'll rendezvous back at the flat DI Mangat. I expect a thorough progress report on FaithHate.

VINCE exits as TARL struggles with GARY.

SIDHU: You expect us to put our exes in your boxes.

JOANNE: I'm very grateful...

SIDHU: *(Shouts.)* Then show us some respect! You think Britannia still rules the bloody waves? Because you come and eat a few chappatis at the Gurdwara you are the bloody Queen?

JOANNE: No...

SIDHU: Then pay attention and start representing your community.

TARL: If she gets hold of me it'll be over.

GARY: He says I have to.

TARL: You want to be in charge remember.

GARY roughly pushes her away. JOANNE and SIDHU exit.

GARY: No I don't! I just want to do my job. I joined the police because I wanted to make a difference. I had high hopes...

TARL: You can make a difference by not taking me. Please Gary, I'm begging you.

GARY: I don't understand what's going on.

TARL: Is your natural instinct to take orders or help others?

GARY slowly backs off.

TARL: Problem is your intentions are confused. You need more work.

GARY: But I've got a job…I'm a police officer.

TARL: What else are you?

GARY: I'm…er…a police officer. And…a Sikh.

TARL: Brown skin shows the uniform off better but it doesn't change anything, so your journey is to learn that you're just part of the system.

GARY: Same as you.

TARL: You won't understand this Gary, but I'm slightly different to you.

GARY: How?

TARL: I'm really real. And you're pretend.

GARY: Eh?

TARL: Like an illusion.

TARL takes GARY'S hand and runs it all over her face, her body.

TARL: What do I feel like to you?

GARY: Fat and squashy…

TARL: Real?

GARY: Course…

He touches her arm.

GARY: This bit's sort of like a…lizard.

He pulls away quickly.

GARY: Careful the reptiles don't chew you up.

TARL exits.

SCENE ELEVEN

Early evening. The MAN enters. Standing by the kitchen unit, he starts wrapping the GIRL's body up in the white sheets, pieces of which are now stained with blood. JOANNE stands opposite ANDREW on the set which represents his office – desk, filing cabinet and chairs. It's as if the two different sets have become integrated but JOANNE and ANDREW do not acknowledge the MAN, nor he them.

ANDREW: This directive's coming from the Home Secretary's people isn't it? *(Shouts.)* Isn't it?

JOANNE: Listen to yourself Andrew, you sound like a paranoid schizophrenic.

ANDREW: Don't tempt me Joanne, I've got a pen knife in my pocket.

JOANNE: Think it through.

The MAN exits. The GIRL's corpse remains on the integrated set.

ANDREW: There's nothing to think about.

JOANNE: Do you ever bother looking out of the window from your ivory tower? Coachloads of youths are arriving from all over the country. Forget the riot, we're facing a potential atrocity.

ANDREW: Let the army deal with it.

JOANNE: They need authorisation from the Home Secretary. He won't, I've checked.

ANDREW: Then any blood that's shed is on his hands.

JOANNE: This is no longer about presenting anal rape and foul language to the converted few. We're risking lives.

ANDREW: Honestly Joanne, this is one of your pathetic ploys isn't it? Atrocity my arse.

JOANNE: Why do you care so much?

ANDREW: Because I'm an artist.

JOANNE: Without this building there are no artists. If this play goes ahead and there's bloodshed, do you suppose anyone in this region's going to support you? In a year your funding will be hacked away and this place will die.

ANDREW: You're putting me in a fucking impossible position!

JOANNE: I'll fight for you. I can build a bridge between you and them, repair the damage.

ANDREW: You promised me.

JOANNE: You've brought the world's media to our city. You've shown that theatre provokes and causes uproar, that it's relevant.

TARLOCHAN enters and observes the kitchen unit. She picks up a tin and reads the label.

TARL: These have got Arabic writing on them. You can't put these in a Gurdwara.

ANDREW: It's just a bit of dressing.

TARL throws the tins and flour onto the floor.

TARL: You should have asked.

ANDREW: Is it really that big a deal?

TARL: This is why they won't believe anything you say, because you never try and understand what you don't know.

JOANNE: Some of us have bigger preoccupations at the moment.

TARL kicks the tins and packets around the space.

The red notebook falls out of her pocket.

ANDREW: Stop that Tarlochan.

TARL: I'm begging you, please get it right.

JOANNE: She encouraged this ridiculous dialogue. Why?

TARL: I thought they might listen…

JOANNE: Why would anybody listen to you?

TARL exits.

JOANNE pointedly turns to ANDREW.

JOANNE: Face it, she hasn't considered your plight for one second.

ANDREW: I don't know what to do.

JOANNE: She'll write other plays, if she's a proper writer she will. In a few months we'll do some juggling with the kitty money and you can take this *Gund* thing on tour.

ANDREW: What will people think of me?

JOANNE: No-one's backing you. Not the police, not the council. If you're going to survive, you and I need to maintain a united front.

ANDREW: You might not even get in next week.

JOANNE: If I don't, you really are fucked. You're dying Andrew, you and your Oxbridge friends. No-one's interested in what you lot think or say any more.

ANDREW: Are you saying that I don't have a point? That I won't stand up for what you know is the right thing to do?

JOANNE: What's stopping you? Go and do it then!

JOANNE picks up the red notebook.

SCENE TWELVE

Lights change. It's as if there is no set and this moment cannot be located. The corpse of the GIRL remains on the floor wrapped in the bloody white sheets. TARL enters and picks up the GIRL as though she is very precious. She regards her lovingly and carries her off.

SCENE THIRTEEN

Evening. The integrated set. KHUSH is slumped down reading the Gund *script. After a few moments TARL enters.*

TARL: Why didn't you burn it, action man?

She grabs the Gund *script from him and he jumps up.*

TARL: It's okay, I knew you weren't capable.

AMRIK enters. TARL puts the script in her pocket.

AMRIK: Good to see you.

TARL: *(In Punjabi.)* I'm ready for you now. How are your mum and dad?

AMRIK doesn't respond.

TARL: No ear for his own language.

AMRIK: You look terrible.

TARL: I eat shit.

AMRIK: Have you finished your script?

TARL: What do you want?

AMRIK: For us to talk. You're not the only one who's got the right to be heard.

TARL turns to KHUSH.

TARL: Back in the day, in the real world, Amrik used to fancy me.

AMRIK: Oh…please…

TARL: I wasn't always this bad looking. We were in youth theatre together. He was in his own way very talented. And kind. But I think that's gone now.

AMRIK: I might not like what you're doing but I care what happens to you.

TARL: Really?

AMRIK: You enjoying your moment in the limelight? Everyone talking about you, saying how concerned they are about your welfare. Won't last much longer. Fleming and his lot might defend your rights and tell you how brave you are but they don't get what you're about. Not like I do.

TARL: They like my writing.

AMRIK: They make you believe you'll rise and shine. But to them you're like a puppy at Christmas and once they've had their fun you'll be back out on the streets again. A little mongrel looking for a new owner. And they'll go in search of a new pet. You won't ever, can't ever be anything more than the exotic ethnic who makes them feel multicultural.

TARL: My play's what matters.

AMRIK: You think putting it on will set you free?

TARL: Yes.

AMRIK: It's destroying you.

TARL: What if you're right? What do I do?

AMRIK: Come back to your people, where you belong.

TARL: What about what's in my head?

AMRIK: You'll be looked after. The filth in your head will go away, won't be any need to write it.

TARL: So…so it will be like it never happened?

AMRIK: Exactly.

TARL: What if I just feel like writing shameful things?

AMRIK: That'll stop and you'll write something worthwhile.

TARL: But don't I need to be free?

AMRIK: No, you need to feel secure. Why don't you let me have a look at the script? We can work on changing it, together.

TARL takes her Gund *script out.*

TARL: And after that, I'll belong again? You'll take me back?

AMRIK: Yes.

TARL: I think…I think…I'd rather give Nick Griffin a blow job.

AMRIK: What are you Tarlochan? What has your life become?

TARL: I like it.

AMRIK: Give me the script.

TARL: The play's going on.

KHUSH: Birji…

TARL: Shut up shit! Hurt people hurt people don't they Amrik? *(To KHUSH.)* Have you met his daughter?

AMRIK: Fuck off.

TARL: *(To KHUSH.)* Do you ever wonder why he's not married? Are you a Gaylord Amrik?

AMRIK: I am getting married. To a girl from India.

TARL: That is…so…you are so predictable. After all the years of fighting talk you end up with a virgin from the village.

TARL'S phone rings. She glances at the number and turns it off.

TARL: I have to go.

AMRIK: I'm warning you…

TARL stands right in front of him.

TARL: Thing is I know you're not a bad man…

She goes to leave.

TARL: See you lot after the show.

She exits. Embarrassed silence.

AMRIK: Did you speak to her?

KHUSH: No. I only walked in a minute before you.

KHUSH glances at a mark on AMRIK'S hand.

KHUSH: What's that mark Birji?

AMRIK: My warrior mark. Got into a fight with a pig at a demo.

MR SIDHU enters. He does a triumphant little dance.

SIDHU: I did it! I only bloody well did it! Joanne says they may even ask me onto the theatre board. The play is stopped. I stopped it the old-fashioned way. I told your boys and they are retreating.

AMRIK rushes to look outside. He turns to KHUSH.

AMRIK: Get on the phone, tell them to come back.

KHUSH: But the play isn't happening.

AMRIK: The protest will go on.

KHUSH: I reckon she needs help.

SIDHU: And a good hard chapair! *(Slap.)*

AMRIK: You don't know her, she's dangerous. What did she say to you back there?

KHUSH: Nothing.

AMRIK: Do you feel the same as you did this morning?

KHUSH: Don't know.

AMRIK: Then she's done a good job. She's persuaded you to doubt everything you truly value. I'm instructing you to carry out my orders, even if you don't feel like it. If you still feel the same way this time tomorrow then do whatever you like. Trust me, brother.

KHUSH: Okay.

AMRIK: Get outside and organise your troops. Hurry! Then I want you back here.

KHUSH: But you don't need me any more.

AMRIK: There's something I want you to observe.

KHUSH runs out.

SIDHU: You are a graceless man Amrik. What has happened to make you so mangled?

AMRIK: I've watched and learned from the Master Uncleji.

MR SIDHU goes to exit.

AMRIK: Where are you going?

SIDHU: To pick up seven kilos of salt cod. The fish samoseh appear to be more of a reality than ever.

AMRIK: They're all laughing at you. Joanne, Fleming, the Home Secretary…

SIDHU: Let them laugh. As long as I get what I want, let them laugh.

SCENE FOURTEEN

Showtime. ANDREW'S office on the integrated set. JOANNE and ANDREW solemnly stand before a shaking TARLOCHAN, she is having a panic attack.

ANDREW: *(Alarmed.)* What's going on?

JOANNE: Panic attack. Teachers have them all the time.

JOANNE reaches for a jug of water on the desk and throws it over TARLOCHAN.

JOANNE: Old trick from the staff room.

TARL: I don't understand.

JOANNE: Circumstances have changed.

ANDREW: It would be irresponsible of me to place the theatre in further jeopardy so I'm afraid the decision has been made for me.

TARL: Is this real?

JOANNE: No writer has the right to frighten a community.

TARL: Has this really happened?

She grabs JOANNE and feels her body all over.

JOANNE: *(Angry.)* Get off me!

TARL: Stand up, sit down, stand up, sit down…

JOANNE: She's lost the plot now.

TARL: So is what's in my head stronger than what's real?

ANDREW: What?

TARL: Or is it the other way around?

JOANNE and ANDREW exchange a weary look.

JOANNE: Maybe it's some sort of bipolar code.

TARL: Please…I need to know…

ANDREW: Just because we can't put *Gund* on at the moment doesn't mean there's no future for the play.

TARL: There's no future.

ANDREW: There's a strong possibility of mounting a co-production with a prime London venue in a few months, you couldn't hope for better exposure...

TARL: Is it because you didn't like the ending?

ANDREW sighs.

TARL: Maybe I can come up with something else.

ANDREW: Oh, Denis Edwards wants to talk to you. Did you see his last play here?

TARL shakes her head.

ANDREW: He's keen on writing a fact-based drama about what's happening to you right now. Apparently there's interest from Radio 4.

TARL: You're a coward.

ANDREW: I'm as much a victim of this situation as you are. I have to consider the welfare of my staff as well as the damage being done to our bricks and mortar by those morons outside.

TARL: Don't call them that.

ANDREW: You call them worse in your play.

TARL: What will you do now? Put on those Enid Blyton Asian plays where everyone loves each other in the end? Get the curry smells wafting through the auditorium while the audience are mesmerised by the singing of wafer thin red and gold dancers. We're not all like that. My life isn't like that.

JOANNE: Perhaps you should ask yourself why it isn't.

ANDREW: I sincerely hope we'll work together again.

ANDREW turns to go.

ANDREW: The press are waiting.

TARL: What do you do Andrew? I can write, what can you do?

He exits.

JOANNE: Has it ever struck you that no-one is particularly interested in what you do?

TARL: Why are all those people outside then?

JOANNE: It's what surrounds what you do that is of interest. Creators have been overtaken by commentators. No-one reads books any more, they read about them, no-one even has any real opinions, they just like to hear them being discussed. It's people who don't actually do anything who set the agenda.

TARL: But if I didn't write the play, no agenda would exist.

JOANNE: The time for writing is over.

JOANNE opens her bag and takes out a hand mirror, she checks her make up.

TARLOCHAN approaches a portable television and turns it on. As before the image is projected onto a screen. ANDREW FLEMING stands on a podium and addresses a bustling press conference.

JOANNE: Don't watch this.

ANDREW: Everyone connected to the Writers' Theatre is very disappointed that the performance is cancelled. But matters have been taken out of my hands. I have personally spoken to Tarlochan and she has specifically requested that the play be pulled. The police have informed her of an increase in threats to her personal safety. The theatre appreciates Tarlochan's fear in these circumstances and we support her right to protect herself. We abhor the violence which has caused damage to the front of the Writers' Theatre building and hope that once the situation in the city has calmed down we can look to producing *Gund...*

TARLOCHAN abruptly turns the television off and the screens go dead. Devastated, she turns to JOANNE.

TARL: Why…why did he say that?

JOANNE: He had to say something.

TARL starts to crumble and shake.

TARL: What am I supposed to do now?

JOANNE: Perhaps you'll use this experience to write a new play.

TARL checks her pocket, it's empty. She starts frantically searching all over the set.

JOANNE: What are you doing?

TARL: I've lost my script.

JOANNE: Don't you get it? No-one's bothered.

TARL: I have to find it.

She rummages around and opens the filing cabinet. The corpse of the girl wrapped in the bloody sheets falls out on top of her. TARL screams in horror.

JOANNE: No-one's listening.

TARL breaks down. JOANNE eyes her coldly.

JOANNE: I was waiting for you to break. You need to be a lot stronger than this, young lady. *(A Beat.)* Maybe it's some sort of bipolar code… He had to say something… The time for writing is over…

Aghast TARL stares at JOANNE.

JOANNE opens her bag as if to take out her mirror. She instead takes out the red notebook, it falls to the floor. TARL picks it up.

JOANNE: Panic attack. Teachers have them all the time. I was waiting for you to break. You need to be a lot stronger than this, young lady… No writer has the right to frighten a community.

SCENE FIFTEEN

TARLOCHAN and SAT are seated in chairs on the integrated set. TARL clutches her red notebook. SAT holds a pad. She flicks through some pages and reads.

SAT: You say you were about four years old. It was the summer holidays and you and your older sister were watching television with your Uncle who had recently arrived from India. You think he was an illegal immigrant. Your sister made fun of the way he walked and spoke. Your Uncle took swigs from a bottle of Johnny Walker Black label. He didn't understand what your sister was saying but after a while he realised she was laughing at him and he punched her. She continued to laugh so he struck her again. He was very angry and he dragged her out of the room, up the stairs. He was shouting and she was screaming. You wanted to go to the toilet but when you tried to open the door you couldn't. He'd locked it. Later that day you remember the house being cleaned by various family members. You never saw your sister again. Your mother was away in India at the time and your family moved out of the area shortly after this incident. From that day on nobody in the family mentioned your sister. Your Uncle now runs a successful minicab business in Vancouver. What was your sister's name?

TARL: Can't remember.

SAT: This would be easier if I put your words on a disc.

TARL: No recording.

SAT: You subsequently retreated to a world of fantasy. You excelled academically, developed a form of obsessive compulsive disorder. One notable psychotic episode at University after which you were allotted a CPN. Father alcoholic. Absent mother. Sexually deviant behaviour from your teens onwards. Worked in a hospital laundry and a butcher's shop. You read cookery books in your spare time and enjoy watching darts.

TARL: That's it.

SAT: Why not go to the police about your sister?

TARL: I said I'd talk. Not answer questions.

SAT: What about the play?

TARLOCHAN gets up to go.

SAT: Why give me an exclusive?

TARL: Feels like I'm dead.

SAT: But you're not.

TARL: You'll burn me alive regardless.

SAT: I don't get it.

TARL: You're the one I hate the most. I want you to have me.

SAT: Have you been telling the truth?

TARL: Does it matter?

SAT: *(A Beat.)* Everything that's happened, it's a shame.

TARLOCHAN stops.

TARL: You know the most terrible things need the most love. But they never get it.

SAT fades out. TARL opens the red notebook and writes on the last page.

SCENE SIXTEEN

TARL is furiously writing on the last page of her notebook. The GIRL'S corpse lies in the middle of the stage. TARL reads out the beginning of Scene 16 to the audience. As she reads the characters do what she says.

TARL: Scene Sixteen. Evening. AMRIK is leaning over the photocopier on the integrated set. KHUSH enters.

KHUSH: Tried to get them back, but they didn't want to stay.

TARL: TARLOCHAN enters with the red notebook. They all look at each other.

TARL stands and they all look at each other.

TARL: This is for you. It's my new script.

She chucks the notebook to AMRIK who catches it. AMRIK takes out a lighter. KHUSH panics.

KHUSH: Don't! There's no need.

AMRIK: I want you to watch me.

KHUSH: I read Gund.

AMRIK: All the more reason.

KHUSH: It's not what we thought.

AMRIK lights up a flame.

KHUSH: At least read it first Birji!

AMRIK opens the notebook and looks at the first page.

AMRIK: *(Reads.)* Behud...

KHUSH: Beyond Belief...

AMRIK sets fire to the notebook. KHUSH tries to put the fire out.

TARL: *(To KHUSH)* Leave him!

The paper burns until it is ash.

TARL: I found a great ending.

AMRIK: Shut up!

TARL: You don't understand Amrik, it's perfect.

AMRIK suddenly fires the gun at TARL but it just sounds a sorry click. AMRIK keeps trying to shoot TARL but keeps failing. TARL lies down next to the GIRL'S corpse and puts her arm around the dead body.

Suddenly the photocopier starts going and sheets of typed paper come out of it and are blown around the set. KHUSH collects pieces of paper together. AMRIK fades out. As the paper continues to come out of the photocopier, it seems like the stage is transforming into a sea of scripts. KHUSH reads the script.

KHUSH: *(Reads.)* Prologue. Dawn. The stage is black. The lights go up slowly to reveal an Asian woman, TARLOCHAN, lying on the floor in front of a plain desk and chair in a huge stark white space.

KHUSH fades out. TARL slowly gets up just as she does at the start of the play. She goes to sit at the desk, picks up a red notebook and starts to write.

THE END